BIRD LIFE IN IRELAND

BIRDWATCHING CAN BE FUN for everyone, children and adults, mountaineers and strollers, stay-at-home types and outdoor enthusiasts. With this book you can get started – and go quite a long way.

The FIRST SECTION orientates you and gives general information. The SECOND SECTION describes the birds you are most likely to see in Ireland, pointing out special features which help identify the bird and listing their habits and general behaviour. With each bird we also list others which are easily confused with that species to help you distinguish between them. The birds here are organised according to taxonomic order, that is, in family groupings.

The COLOUR PLATES present the birds as you are likely to see them in their habitats.

In the THIRD SECTION you are given suggestions for trips all over Ireland to places which are famous for birds.

**This book can open your eyes to a whole
new way of seeing the world.**

D0916058

BIRD LIFE
IN IRELAND

Jim Wilson & Don Conroy

THE O'BRIEN PRESS
DUBLIN

First published 1994 by The O'Brien Press, Ltd.,
20 Victoria Road, Rathgar, Dublin 6, Ireland.

Copyright © Jim Wilson and Don Conroy

All rights reserved. No part of this book may be reproduced or utilised in
any form or by any means, including photocopying, recording
or by any information storage and retrieval system without permission in
writing from the publisher. This book may not be sold
as a bargain book or at a reduced rate without
permission in writing from the publisher.

British Library Cataloguing-in-publication Data
Conroy, Don, Birdlife in Ireland
I. Title II. Wilson, Jim
598.0723415

ISBN 0-86278-396-8

The O'Brien Press receives assistance from
The Arts Council/An Chomhairle Ealaíon.

2 4 6 8 10 9 7 5 3 1
96 98 00 02 04 03 01 99 97 95

Cover illustrations: Don Conroy
Cover design: The O'Brien Press
Photo, back cover: Joe Wilson
Typesetting, editing, layout: The O'Brien Press
Printing: The Guernsey Press Co. Ltd.

Contents

ACKNOWLEDGEMENTS

Ann, Peter, Barry, Mom and Dad, Clive Hutchinson, Pat Smiddy, John O'Halloran, Staff of the Irish Wildbird Conservancy (IWC) and the Royal Society for the Protection of Birds (RSPB, Northern Ireland), Sean Pierce and Barry O'Mahony, Ian Burrows and Steve Yeo, Margaret O'Leary, Tim Cadogan, Sheila Carmody, Terry Carruthers, Chris Wilson, John Marsh, John Murphy, Ralph Sheppard, Sean Corry, Mary Durkin, Oran O'Sullivan, Gay Conroy, Gabriel King, Michael O'Brien, Dermod Lynskey, ENFO, RTE, Leo Hallissey, Dick Warner, Derek Mooney, IPCC, Killian Mullarney, David Daly. All in Cape Clear, especially Mary O'Donoghue. Our friends for encouragement and all those who had a positive influence on our birdwatching over the last twenty years.

List of Birds

This list can also function as a checklist, so you can mark off the birds you have spotted. Birds are listed here in alphabetical order to help you find the species you want. The text on species in the book is structured according to *taxonomic* order. The colour plates are organised according to *habitat*.

- [ ] Jackdaw (*Corvus monedula*) 166
- [ ] Kestrel (*Falco tinnunculus*) 116
- [ ] Kingfisher (*Alcedo atthis*) 142
- [ ] Lapwing (*Vanellus vanellus*) 123
- [ ] Linnet (*Carduelis cannabina*) 176
- [ ] Little Grebe (*Tachybaptus ruficollis*) 103
- [ ] Long-eared Owl (*Asio otus*) 140
- [ ] Long-tailed Tit (*Aegithalos caudatus*) 162
- [ ] Magpie (*Pica pica*) 165
- [ ] Mallard (*Anas platyrhynchos*) 113
- [ ] Meadow Pipit (*Anthus pratensis*) 147
- [ ] Mistle Thrush (*Turdus viscivorus*) 156
- [ ] Moorhen (*Gallinula chloropus*) 120
- [ ] Mute Swan (*Cygnus olor*) 108
- [ ] Oystercatcher (*Haematopus ostralegus*) 121
- [ ] Peregrine (*Falco peregrinus*) 116
- [ ] Pheasant (*Phasianus colchicus*) 117
- [ ] Pied Wagtail (*Motacilla alba*) 149
- [ ] Raven (*Corvus corax*) 169
- [ ] Razorbill (*Alca torda*) 135
- [ ] Red-breasted Merganser (*Mergus serrator*) 114
- [ ] Redpoll (*Carduelis flammea*) 177
- [ ] Redshank (*Tringa totanus*) 127
- [ ] Reed Bunting (*Emberiza schoeniclus*) 180
- [ ] Ringed Plover (*Charadrius hiaticula*) 122
- [ ] Robin (*Erithacus rubecula*) 152
- [ ] Rock Pipit (*Anthus petrosus*) 148
- [ ] Rook (*Corvus frugilegus*) 167

- [ ] Sand Martin (*Riparia riparia*) 144
- [ ] Sandwich Tern (*Sterna sandvicensis*) 131
- [ ] Sedge Warbler (*Acrocephalus schoenobaenus*) 157
- [ ] Shag (*Phalacrocorax aristotelis*) 107
- [ ] Shelduck (*Tadorna tadorna*) 110
- [ ] Short-eared Owl (*Asio flammeus*) 141
- [ ] Siskin (*Carduelis spinus*) 175
- [ ] Skylark (*Alauda arvensis*) 143
- [ ] Snipe (*Gallinago gallinago*) 125
- [ ] Song Thrush (*Turdus philomelos*) 155
- [ ] Sparrowhawk (*Accipter nisus*) 115
- [ ] Spotted Flycatcher (*Muscicapa striata*) 161
- [ ] Starling (*Sturnus vulgaris*) 170
- [ ] Stonechat (*Saxicola torquata*) 153
- [ ] Swallow (*Hirundo rustica*) 145
- [ ] Swift (*Apus apus*) 141
- [ ] Teal (*Anas crecca*) 112
- [ ] Tufted Duck (*Aythya fuligula*) 113
- [ ] Turnstone (*Arenaria intertres*) 127
- [ ] Water Rail (*Rallus aquaticus*) 118
- [ ] Wigeon (*Anas penelope*) 111
- [ ] Willow Warbler (*Phylloscopus trochilus*) 159
- [ ] Woodpigeon (*Columba palumbus*) 135
- [ ] Wren (*Troglodytes troglodytes*) 151
- [ ] Yellowhammer (*Emberiza citrinella*) 179

Introduction

This book is designed to provide a general introduction to birds and birdwatching in Ireland. It gives practical advice on how to get to know the birdlife that surrounds us. It is written for people who know very little about Irish birds but would like to know more or who would like to make the study of birds their hobby – an interest that will last a lifetime and will always be full of surprises. Technical jargon is avoided wherever possible and, apart from one or two exceptions, scarce and rare birds are not dealt with. The book will be a continuing source of reference on our common birds, and unlike many other guides it deals exclusively with the birdlife of the whole island of Ireland.

Who Can Become a Birdwatcher?

Birdwatching might, on the surface, seem to be a pastime for a few strange people running around the countryside looking for small brown birds. In fact, we are all birdwatchers to a greater or lesser degree, whether we are looking at a cheeky robin in the garden, listening to seagulls at the beach in summer or feeding the swans at the local pond.

Birdwatching (and listening!) can become a lifetime hobby. No special equipment is needed, though a pair of binoculars will broaden your horizons immensely. The basic requirement is at least one good eye or one good ear, nothing else. Birdwatching is a hobby suitable either for a group or for the individual wanting to get away from it all. The beauty of birdwatching is that birds are everywhere, from the windowsill in the centre of a town or city to the most remote, windswept island.

So you can birdwatch anywhere, any time. Requirements for birdwatching are independent of age, sex or physical ability. Even if you are confined to home, to bed, or to a wheelchair, you are in business as long as you have even the most limited opening to the outside world.

Once you are bitten by the bug (or bird!), there is no limit to the amount of knowledge to be gained from studying even one bird species. Whole books have been written about the robin alone. By taking part in national and international surveys, getting involved in practical conservation work or just admiring the variety of form and beauty of our feathered friends, even amateurs can make a valuable contribution to our knowledge and the conservation of birds.

Birdwatching is one of the best introductions, for young and old alike, to the natural world around us. You may find that your attention will be drawn to flowers and plants which birds use or to the multitude of creatures, big and small, on which they prey or which prey on them. Most good birdwatchers are also very knowledgeable about plants, animals, butterflies and moths, and even weather forecasting! Many of the most famous naturalists began as birdwatchers.

What Are Birds?

Birds are a group of animals characterised by the fact that they all have feathers, a feature not found in any other group. Flight is an ability shared with a few mammals, among other creatures, but it is argued that it is in birds that the art of flying is at its best.

An examination of the structure of a bird would suggest that birds are descended from either dinosaurs or lizards, retaining features of both these groups, such as laying eggs and having reptilian scales on their legs. Current theories suggest that dinosaurs, lizards and birds are all descended from a common ancestor.

One famous bird fossil is that of archaeopteryx, which lived 150 million years ago. Recently, even older bird fossils have been discovered, showing that these masters of the air have been flying around for a very long time.

There are over 8,000 species (different types) of bird in the world and it is hard to believe that even to this day new species are being discovered. Unfortunately, man has been responsible for the extinction of over 200 bird species in the last 300 years.

Birds come in all shapes and sizes: 1. swallow, 2. swift, 3. kestrel, 4. skylark, 5. curlew, 6. barn owl, 7. pheasant, 8. lapwing.

Many of these birds were either flightless or were restricted to islands, particularly in the southern hemisphere. They became extinct due to overhunting by humans or because predators such as cats, dogs, goats and rats came to these isolated areas with man.

One of the most famous recent extinctions (June 1844) was that of the great auk, a goose-sized flightless seabird – the last great auk seen in Ireland had been captured off the coast of Waterford just ten years before. Birds that once bred in Ireland include the golden eagle and the white-tailed eagle. These extinctions serve to show us how the future and diversity of birdlife on this planet lies firmly in our hands, and it is up to us (not somebody else) to ensure that this wonderful diversity is maintained.

Where and How Do Birds Live in Ireland?

A general rule for animals is that larger land masses have a greater number of species. Larger areas of land have a greater range of climate, vegetation and topography (physical features). Hence they have more habitats. Ireland is a small island with fewer breeding species (133) than Britain (190) or France (260). The total number of breeding bird species in Europe, excluding Russia, is approximately 420.

No matter where you live on this island birds are not very far away. They have learned to live with man and many species have thrived as a result of our activities.

Bird species have diversified by adapting to different habitats or niches. As a result, they can be divided into different groups based on how and where they live. People who study how bird species are related to each other are called bird taxonomists. They have divided bird species into families based on similarities of certain features of their body structure. Some birds which might look similar, such as penguins and auks, are not in fact closely related, as is shown by closer study. They have evolved to look alike because they live in similar habitats. Other birds may look totally different, for example the robin and the blue tit, but are, in fact, closely related. Closely-related families are put together in groups or orders.

Latin is the universal language of zoology, the study of all living things. It allows people from different countries to be sure they are talking about the same creature. For example, a robin in Ireland and a robin in America are two totally different species. This is not obvious from their English name but it is from their Latin names. No two species have the same Latin name. The Latin name for groups or orders of birds always ends in *-iformes,* and where and how birds live in Ireland is discussed under these headings below.

NOTE: The number in brackets indicates the number of species of each group seen in Ireland up to July 1994.

Divers *Gaviiformes* (4)

These birds spend most of their time on the water and catch their food by diving. They are able to stay underwater for long periods of time. They very rarely breed in Ireland and are mainly winter visitors around our coast.

Grebes *Podicipediformes* (6)

These include grebes and also water birds which dive for their food. They are more common than the divers and are regularly seen on the coast and also inland on ponds and lakes.

15

Fulmar, Petrels, Shearwaters ...
Procellariiformes
(14)

Birds in this group spend most of their time on the open sea. They include the fulmar and the storm petrel. Shearwaters, which are also in this group, nest in burrows on remote islands, coming ashore only at night to avoid predators. They have poorly-developed leg muscles for walking and would therefore be vulnerable to attack on land. Ireland is a very important location for this group of birds.

Gannet, Cormorants, Shag ...
Pelecaniformes **(3)**

As the Latin name suggests, birds

in this group are related to the pelican. All are fish-eaters.

Herons, Egrets ... *Ciconiiformes* **(15)**

The grey heron is the only common representative of this group in Ireland. Almost all members of this group have powerful beaks and long legs. Little egrets, once shot for their brilliant white

plumage, are being seen here in increasing numbers in recent years. The bittern, also a member of this group, was once a common breeding bird in Ireland. It became extinct here in the middle of the 19th century and now appears here only as a rare migrant.

Swans, Geese, Ducks ... *Anseriformes* (45)

This group of water birds is well-represented in Ireland. The ducks can be divided into two main sections – those that feed from the surface of the water, sometimes called 'dabbling ducks', such as the mallard and teal, and those that dive underwater to catch their food, such as the tufted duck. The Wexford wildfowl refuge, on the North Slob, is internationally important for the Greenland white-fronted goose, emblem of the Irish Wildbird Conservancy (IWC). Each winter over 40 percent of the total world population of this species come to the reserve. We have three swan species in Ireland – the well-known mute swan and also the whooper and Bewick's swan which are winter visitors and often referred to as wild swans. (See also chapter on folklore).

Hawks, Falcons, Vultures, Eagles ...
Falconiformes (22)

Hawks and falcons are the most common members of this group in Ireland. The only official record of a wild vulture in Ireland was of one caught alive near Cork harbour in the spring of 1843. Our eagles were hunted to extinction, though the occasional migrant is still seen. A re-introduction programme for the white-tailed eagle is in progress in Munster. The buzzard is increasing in numbers, spreading south from the north-east.

Pheasant, 'Game Birds' ... *Galliformes* (6)

The only common member of this group in Ireland is the pheasant, which was brought here in the 16th century. All members of this group in Ireland are referred to as 'game birds'. This is because they are either hunted today or were hunted in the past.

Cranes, Rails, Crakes, Moorhen, Coots ... *Gruiformes* (13)

Most members of this group live in or near wet areas with tall dense vegetation. The corncrake, once very common all over Ireland, is now on the brink of extinction. The IWC and the Royal Society for the Protection of Birds (RSPB), with cooperation from the Office of Public Works(OPW), the Department of the Environment (DOE) and the international bird conservation organisation Birdlife International, are attempting to save this species from extinction in Ireland through land purchase and management and by advocating corncrake-friendly farming practices.

Waders, Skuas, Gulls, Terns, Auks
Charadriiformes (104)

After the perching birds, this is the largest and arguably one of the most important group of birds in Ireland. It includes waders such as the oystercatcher, plover, snipe and sandpipers; also skuas, gulls, terns and auks. Every winter our wetlands become the feeding grounds for hundreds of thousands of waders. During the short winter days they spend most of their time on mud or sand, feeding on a variety of small creatures that live on or near the surface. Some feed almost 24 hours a day, stopping only when the tide covers their feeding grounds. They normally feed in flocks ranging from just a few birds to thousands. When a large flock of waders, such as dunlin or golden plover, takes to the sky, they fly over the estuary as a unit, turning and twisting in unison. They will bank from side to side, flashing their pale undersides, beginning at the front of the flock and spreading along its length. This movement is called 'wheeling', and provides a kind of natural firework display, difficult to surpass.

The birds' bills have developed in various ways to exploit the different types of prey on which they feed, thus avoiding competition for the same food source. Some, such as the plovers, feed by sight and have very short bills, while others use their sense of touch and feel their prey below the surface, usually with long, thin and often curved bills. Ireland is internationally important for waders, with large numbers coming here each winter from their breeding grounds in northern Europe and Russia. Only small numbers breed in Ireland and so in the summer months our estuaries are almost completely deserted. The birds' wintering and breeding grounds here are coming under increasing pressure from 'development'. We have an international obligation to protect these birds and their habitats.

Skuas are mainly non-breeding summer visitors and are often referred to as sea-hawks or pirates. They chase other seabirds, usually gulls and terns, until they surrender the food they are carrying.

Gulls are found everywhere in Ireland, from the inland-nesting black-headed gull to the great black-backed gull found mainly on cliffs and offshore islands. They have adapted to living with man. Two examples of this are the noisy clouds of scavenging gulls at a refuse tip and the trail of gulls following the plough in search of insects and worms.

Terns come here in their thousands each summer from their wintering grounds in Africa and beyond. The roseate tern, which is the rarest breeding tern in Europe, has one of its largest colonies on the IWC/OPW-managed island of Rockabill off the north Dublin coast.

Auks are represented by only a few species in Ireland, but they more than make up for this in numbers, especially in the breeding season when hundreds of thousands of them cram onto cliff ledges around the coast.

Doves, Pigeons ... *Columbiformes* **(6)**

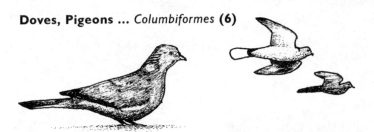

These birds are characterised by very short legs, small heads and cooing calls. The most common member of this group is the woodpigeon, which can be a serious pest to farmers. The most recent arrival is the collared dove, unheard of here before 1959, and now widespread and common.

Cuckoos *Cuculiformes* (4)

Four cuckoo species have been recorded in Ireland. The most common is the cuckoo, which comes  here every summer and lays its eggs in another bird's nest, leaving the foster parents to raise their outsized lodger.

One south European and two American species of cuckoo have also been reported in Ireland.

Owls *Strigiformes* (6)

Six members of this group have occurred in Ireland, but only two – the barn owl and the long-eared owl – regu-  larly breed here. The short-eared owl is a scarce winter visitor and the other three are very rare. They mainly feed on rats, mice, voles and small birds.

Nightjars *Caprimulgiformes* (1)

Only one member of this group is found in Ireland. This is the nightjar, an insect-eating summer visitor from Africa. It is very scarce, nesting usually in open wood-land. Like other members of this group, it is nocturnal. It has long wings and tail, and its plumage provides perfect camouflage during the day when it is resting on the ground or in a tree.

Swifts *Apodiformes* **(5)**

The swift is the only member of this group commonly found in Ireland – the other four are very rare. The swift is a summer visitor, coming here only to lay its eggs and rear its young under the eaves of big buildings. Like the other members of this group, it catches its staple diet of insects by flying quickly through the air with its large mouth open, each bird catching tens of thousands of insects each summer.

Kingfishers, Hoopoes ...
Coraciiformes **(5)**

By far the most colourful group of birds visiting our shores. The most famous is the diminutive kingfisher. Other members of this group, found in Ireland, are the hoopoe, which is seen in small numbers, usually in the spring, the belted kingfisher, an extremely rare visitor from America, and the very rare bee-eater and roller.

Woodpeckers *Piciformes* (5)

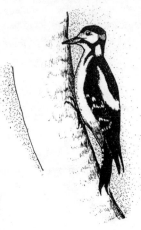

Woodpeckers are very rare visitors to Ireland, despite the fact that four species breed as close as Britain. The main reason is that they do not usually migrate. It is thought that Ireland became cut off from Britain and the rest of Europe before woodpeckers had a chance to colonise this island. There is also a suggestion that they became extinct following the removal of our forests. In fact, two of the five species on record are from North America, where some woodpeckers do migrate, while a number of European species, breeding much closer to Ireland, have yet to be seen here.

Pipits, Thrushes, Warblers, Crows, Finches, Buntings ... *Passeriformes* (154)

This is the largest group of birds in Ireland. 'Passerines' include many varieties of perching birds that live on dry land. They normally feed on insects, seeds or berries. Like the other groups described, many do not move far, while some are highly migratory.

Passerines are represented in almost every habitat in Ireland, from the meadow pipit which can breed at high altitudes to the migratory warblers that come in summer to feed their young on the myriad insects in our woodland canopies. This group also includes the thrushes, some of which are resident species while others are winter visitors. The finches and buntings feed on insects in the breeding season and mainly on seeds in the winter. Crows are also in this group, and can be described as the 'vultures of Ireland'. Most foreign birdwatchers visiting this island will comment on the large number of crows. Even the common rook, which we take for granted, is less numerous in countries as close as Holland. Their ability to take advantage of man's activities and their adaptability has made them one of the most successful bird groups in Ireland.

Birds in Irish Folklore

Long before binoculars, telescopes and cameras, people in Ireland were watching birds. They hunted them for food, used their feathers for decoration and carefully observed their habits to explain some of the mysteries of their world. They also used them to mark the seasons – the arrival of the first swallows heralding summer and the arrival of the wild swans and geese telling of winter's approach. There is much evidence in our art and culture to show that birds played an important part in the lives of our ancestors.

In many pre-Christian Irish legends 'wild' swans (whooper or Bewick's) appear. In County Mayo, it was thought that the souls of virtuous women lived in the swans. Anyone who interfered with the swans would die before the end of the year. To this day most people have a reverence for swans. From Lough Inchiquin in County Clare, there is a story that the chieftain of the Quins, who had a castle on the lake, married a mysterious woman whom he found in a nearby cave. She told him that no O'Brien must ever enter the castle. One day an O'Brien did enter the castle and the woman and her children immediately jumped into the lake and turned into swans.

In 'The Wooing of Etaine', written down in the eighth century, Midir appeared in the banqueting hall, 'while Tara was surrounded by all the champions of Ireland, ring within ring'. He had come to claim his prize for beating King Eochaid in a game of chess – to hold his wife Etaine in his arms. He held his weapons in his left hand and Etaine in his right and rose up through the smoke hole in the hall. The assembled crowd saw them as two white swans circling Tara. After nine years hiding in a fairy mound King Eochaid regained Etaine and returned home in triumph. There is a very strong similarity between this tale and one found in Indian culture.

There are numerous references to birds in the legends of Cú Chulainn. In one story Cú Chulainn was attending the festival of Samhain and a flock of the most beautiful birds landed on the nearby lake. In true heroic fashion, he slew them all and gave one to every woman of the court except his wife. Obviously she was not at all happy about this, and to soothe her he promised that the next time the birds came he would kill the two loveliest for her. Soon two birds appeared on the lake, linked with chains of red gold. They sang so sweetly that everyone present fell asleep. Despite his best efforts, Cú Chulainn could not slay the birds. The motif of swans joined by gold or silver chains is found in many countries such as Tibet, Greece, Persia, Germany, France, England and Scotland, and is therefore thought to be ancient in origin and possibly having a magical or ritual connection.

The most famous story concerning swans in Ireland is 'The Children of Lir'. The king's daughter and three sons were trans-

formed into swans by their wicked step-mother and doomed to spend nine hundred years on lake and sea. They sang such magical music that a spell fell on all who heard them and flocks of birds gathered round to listen. After the time had passed, the swans found sanctuary with a Christian monk and were transformed back into their human form. They were now very old and frail and were baptised just before they died. This story has its roots in much older legends such as that of Oengus, son of the god Dagda.

Birds with black plumage, especially members of the crow family, have always been associated with evil and death. In Celtic legends the raven was considered to be a messenger of the enemy and there is a saying that 'he is in the book of the black raven', meaning he is not to be trusted. In the Bible, the raven was the first bird sent out from the ark by Noah. Lug, the father of Cú Chulainn, was a god and was frequently linked with the raven. The observation that scavenging crows will eat eyes is personified in Lug, who was described as going around 'on one foot and with one eye' chanting incantations.

The war-goddess, the Badhbh Catha (Raven of Battle) appeared to Cú Chulainn. When dying, Cú Chulainn tied himself to a stone in the field of battle to defy his enemies. Only when a crow landed on his shoulder did his enemies know he was dead, for no bird would have dared to do this if he were alive. Today most people think that the bird that landed on Cú Chulainn's shoulder was a raven, but there are other accounts that suggest it might have been a hooded crow or even a hawk.

The magpie, which came to Ireland only at the end of the seventh century, is thought by some cultures to bring good luck and by others bad luck. Here in Ireland it is thought that the raven was the bird originally credited with these powers, later transferred to the magpie. One version of a popular rhyme is as follows:

> *One for sorrow,*
> *Two for joy,*
> *Three for a girl,*
> *Four for a boy,*
> *Five for silver,*
> *Six for gold,*
> *Seven for a secret never to be told.*

It is even said that the unassuming pied wagtail has a drop of the devil's blood in it, because of its black and white plumage.

Birds and bird calls have long been used to explain mysterious noises at night and are also associated with the little people and fairies. In Northern Ireland the word 'whaup' is another word for

a curlew, which can often be heard calling at night. It is also the name of a goblin with a long beak which is said to move about under the eaves of houses at night. The calls of a water rail heard from a dark bog road must surely have been the inspiration for many of the fantastic creatures thought to live in such places.

The wren is well-represented in Irish folklore, its cult dating back to the Bronze Age megalithic tomb builders. It was considered to have great powers and was referred to as the 'druid bird'.

The cleverness of the wren is described in the legend of a flying competition where the wren hid on the back of the eagle and, by soaring upwards when the eagle could fly no higher, flew the highest and so became the king of all birds. In one Celtic version of this story – a story found in many cultures around the world – the eagle was so annoyed with the wren that it snapped off part of its tail and so the wren has had to fly low ever since. Evidence of the wren's importance in early times was found at a ring fort in County Cork where a tiny, beautiful ornament, closely resembling the shape of a wren, was unearthed and was dated to the sixth century. In the legend of St Moling, he cursed the wren for eating his pet fly and proclaimed: 'Let children and young persons be destroying him.'

The wren was once – and in some places still is – hunted and killed a few days before St Stephen's Day. In some parts of the country if a wren could not be found, other small birds were used. In areas where the killing of the wren is not approved of nowadays, substitutes are used, such as a potato decorated with feathers to resemble a wren. In fact, today the killing of the wren and other small birds is illegal.

The 'Wren Boys', carrying their mock or slain bird, go 'on the wran' from house to house in fancy dress, usually with faces blackened, wearing such things as women's dresses, scarves, all types of head gear and Wellington boots. The wren is carried on a holly branch or in a container, ranging in design and quality from a hollowed-out turnip to a specially-designed box. When the occupant of the house answers the door, the Wren Boys sing a short verse in return for some money. There are different versions of this song, in both English and Irish, sung to a similar tune with words similar to the following verse:

> *The wren*, the wren that you may see*
> *Is guarded up in a holly tree,*
> *a bunch of ribbons by its side*
> *and (householder's name) to be his guide.*
> *Hurrah, me boys, Hurrah!*
> *Up with the kettles and down with the pots,*
> *give us your answer and let us be gone.*
> *Hurrah, me boys, Hurrah!*

(*Sometimes pronounced 'wran')

31

The eagle represents St John and also the resurrection and ascension of Jesus. It was thought that the eagle, alone of all living creatures, could look into the sun and not be dazzled.

After the procession, the wren's body is thrown away, buried near the house of a disliked person or, as in parts of County Clare, buried outside the house of the person who treated the Wren Boys most generously.

The money collected is usually used to fund a dance that evening. Today, where the custom still survives, it is often used to collect funds for charity. The tradition of killing the wren has all but disappeared and even the singing of the wren song is fast becoming a thing of the past.

Other birds are associated with the Irish Christian tradition. The robin is said to have got its red breast from the blood of Jesus

Christ while standing under his cross. Birds appear in early Christian art, for example on high crosses and in illuminated manuscripts such as the Book of Kells. Barnacle geese were believed to be more fish than fowl, developing from goose barnacles, and so could be eaten during Lent.

A robin that comes inside the house is considered good luck in most parts of the island. Rooks nesting near a house portend good luck. If they desert their nests, it is a sign of bad luck. Seagulls moving inland predict bad weather and lapwings flying low are a sign of a storm coming. Swallows flying low forecast rain. It is said that when you hear the first cuckoo of the year you should stand still for a moment, then lift your right foot and under it will be a hair the colour of that of a future husband or wife. To find a white hair is considered very lucky.

Finally, birds' names have become part of place-names, probably because particular species or groups were regularly seen at certain places. The Irish word for bird is *éan* and is found in names like Ardnaneane and Rathnaneane in County Limerick, meaning, respectively, 'the hill and fort of the birds'. Proof of how common the eagle was in Ireland is to be found in many place-names throughout the country. *Iolar* is the Irish word for eagle. The anglicised versions of place-names include endings such as -iller, -ilra, and -ulra, as in Slieveanilra, 'the mountain of the eagle', in County Clare; Coumanillar, 'the eagle's hollow', on Keeper's Hill in County Tipperary; Drumiller, 'the ridge of the eagle', in Cavan; and Craiganuller, 'the eagle's rock', on the Tyrone/Derry border.

The Irish word for crow, *préachán,* also features in places such as Knockaphreaghaun in Counties Cork, Clare and Galway. The Irish for raven is *fiach* and is found in the plural form in names such as Mullynaveagh in Tyrone and Glenveagh in Donegal.

The Irish word for a grey heron or crane is *corr*, hence the name Corlough, 'the lake of the heron', found in several townlands and lakes in different counties. Like the eagle, the once-common but now endangered corncrake might be remembered in future in Ireland only in place-names. Its Irish name is *tradhnach* or *tréanach*. Coolatreane in Fermanagh means the meadow of the corncrake; Lugatryna in Wicklow means the corncrake's hollow. In the west and north-west, it is often called *tradhlach* and is found in Carrowtreila in Mayo and Carrowntryla in Galway and Roscommon, meaning the quarter-land of the corncrake.

The cuckoo (cuach) gives its name to Derrycoogh, meaning 'the oak grove of the cuckoo', in County Tipperary. The blackbird (lon) appears in Kilnalun, meaning 'the wood of the blackbirds'. The song thrush (smólach) is found in Glenasmole, 'the valley of the thrushes', near Dublin. The skylark (fuiseóg) is found in Rathnafushogue, 'the fort of the larks', in Carlow. Finally, the Irish word for a bird's nest is nead, and this word is found in many place names, such as Nedeen, 'little nest', the name frequently given to Kenmare in County Kerry. Nadanuller, 'the eagle's nest', is found in many parts of the country, and Derrynaned in Mayo means 'the oak-wood of the birds' nest'.

THINGS TO DO

Examine a map of your own locality and see if any of the names discussed above can be found. Ask parents, grandparents or older people in your area if they remember any local names of places with bird or animal names in them.

Twenty Questions about Irish Birds

1. Which is a bigger threat to small songbirds — magpies or cats?

Much study has been carried out to answer this question and no evidence has been found to support the idea that magpies are the greater culprits. In fact, recent studies have shown that, especially in towns and cities, when the number of songbirds increased or decreased, so too did the number of magpies.

A much greater threat to small songbirds is the cat. Each year, millions of birds are killed by cats in Ireland, far more than those killed by the magpie. Dr. A. Whilde reported in the *Irish Naturalists Journal* that two rural domestic cats in Galway killed 342 small mammals and 128 birds from August 1989 to December 1992.

It is estimated that there is one cat for every ten people in Ireland. That makes the Irish cat population 500,000. If each cat in Ireland caught only one quarter the number killed by the Galway cats it would amount to 2,500,000 birds killed each year! This does not include injured or maimed birds, or those killed but not discovered.

2. What is the largest Irish wild bird?

The largest bird in Ireland is the mute swan, weighing up to 12kg. The first mention of the mute swan in Ireland is as recent as 1750, by Smith in his *History of Cork*. The whooper and Bewick's swans, which come to us from Iceland and Scandinavia, would probably have a better claim to the title as they have been seen in Ireland each winter for thousands of years.

3. What is Ireland's tallest wild bird?

Standing over 1.2 metres high, the grey heron is Ireland's tallest bird. It uses its long, sharp bill, long neck and long legs to catch its prey on lake edges, by the seashore and in streams and rivers. Sometimes it is called the crane because of its shape, though there is another bird called the crane which is a rare visitor to Ireland from continental Europe and has a similar shape to the grey heron.

4. What is Ireland's smallest bird?

The answer is, in fact, the goldcrest and not the wren (as many people assume). At nine centimetres long, the goldcrest is half a centimetre smaller than the wren. It is also Ireland's lightest bird and weighs on average only 5.5 grammes, which means that you would need over 180 goldcrests to match the weight of an ordinary (1kg) bag of sugar.

5. What is Ireland's fastest bird?

It is the peregrine falcon, a scarce breeding bird of prey which has been clocked at over 300 kilometres per hour when 'stooping' – dropping from a height onto its prey with wings held close to its sides. During the 1960s, this bird almost became extinct in Ireland and

elsewhere in Europe due to the use of the chemical DDT for killing insects. The peregrines ate birds that fed on insects poisoned by the DDT and they themselves suffered. Thankfully, DDT and similar chemicals are now banned and the peregrine is becoming more common again.

6. Are birds dinosaurs?

Recent studies of the fossil remains of dinosaurs have led scientists to believe that the birds of today are the closest living relatives of dinosaurs, not directly descended from them but sharing a common ancestor. Like birds, dinosaurs are thought to have been warm-blooded and to have laid eggs. Some dinosaurs, such as the ptero-saurs, were able to glide.

7. Why do birds build nests?

They do so to protect their fragile eggs and their chicks when they hatch. Most birds, especially the smaller ones, use their nest only once, while bigger birds, such as hawks and herons, can use the same nest for many years. The mute swan builds the largest nest of any Irish bird. Some birds, such as the house sparrow and long-eared owl, use the nests of other species, making their own modifications. The razorbill and guillemot do not build nests at all but lay their eggs on bare cliff ledges. Their eggs are rounded at one end and taper to a point at the other and so will roll around in circles if disturbed, instead of going over the edge.

8. What is migration and how and why do birds migrate?

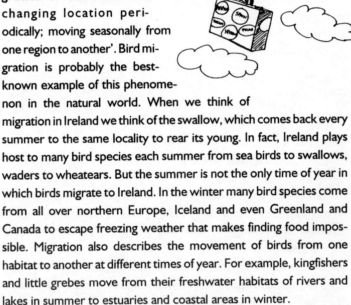

The dictionary definition of migration is 'the action of changing location periodically; moving seasonally from one region to another'. Bird migration is probably the best-known example of this phenomenon in the natural world. When we think of migration in Ireland we think of the swallow, which comes back every summer to the same locality to rear its young. In fact, Ireland plays host to many bird species each summer from sea birds to swallows, waders to wheatears. But the summer is not the only time of year in which birds migrate to Ireland. In the winter many bird species come from all over northern Europe, Iceland and even Greenland and Canada to escape freezing weather that makes finding food impossible. Migration also describes the movement of birds from one habitat to another at different times of year. For example, kingfishers and little grebes move from their freshwater habitats of rivers and lakes in summer to estuaries and coastal areas in winter.

One of the main reasons for bird migration is to find food. Swallows, swifts and many other birds travel over 10,000 kilometres each summer because there are plenty of insects here to feed their young. Many seabirds, such as the common tern and the gannet, come to our shores each summer in their thousands to feed their hungry young on fish caught off our coast. Towards the end of the year, when the insects and fish have all but disappeared, they migrate to Africa where the days are longer and there is enough food to see them through the winter. Ireland is also very important as a 'stepping stone' and 'fuel station' for hundreds of thousands of birds going to countries north of Ireland to breed in the spring and returning south in the autumn.

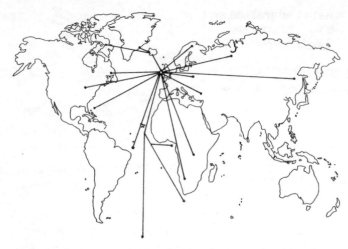

Distances travelled by some of our common and rare migrants.

We have still a lot to learn about migration. It is thought that the urge to migrate is triggered by the length of day, while a change in hormone balance triggers the beginning of preparations for the long journeys that birds undertake. The sedge warbler, for example, will almost double its weight with fat to fuel its long journey. Many small birds can fly non-stop for 2,000 kilometres in less than four days. They find their way using a number of methods, including the stars, familiar geographical features and even the earth's magnetic field. The Arctic tern, the marathon bird of migration, can travel over 250,000 kilometres in its lifetime of migration.

9. Do birds have ears?

Yes, all birds have ears. They are located behind the eyes and are usually covered by feathers, called the ear coverts. Most birds can hear as well as humans but are not so good at hearing high-pitched sounds. Owls have the best hearing of all birds and are better at locating the source of sounds than man. Some species of bird are even able to move their ears.

10. What is an 'albino' bird and are they common?

Generally an albino or partly-albino bird has all or some of its normal coloured feathers replaced by white ones. This is caused by a total loss of colour pigment in some or all of the feathers. Albinism can be genetically inherited or can occur because of injury, shock or bad diet. It appears to be more common in social or sedentary species. Albinos usually do not survive as long as normal birds because they are more conspicuous and vulnerable to predators. True albino birds are rare and not only have white feathers but red eyes and pink skin, bill and legs. Part-albino birds occur twice as often as total albinos. While albinism in dark birds will be more noticeable than in light ones, certain families of birds appear to be more susceptible. One-third of all reported cases of partial or total albinism in birds occurs in the thrush family, particularly in blackbirds. The crow family is next with one-tenth, followed by finches and then other birds. Beware! Birds that roost together will sometimes end up with white bird droppings on some of their feathers and, if they have not washed, can look partly albino.

Other rare conditions that occur are *melanism*, in which an over-production of pigment causes the feathers to look darker than usual, and *leucism* where pigment production is reduced but not stopped, resulting in the plumage colours looking pale or washed out.

11. Why do some birds hop and some birds walk or run?

Birds that spend a lot of their lives in trees, e.g. the chaffinch and robin, have to use both legs to hold on to branches when moving about. They adopt the same movement on the ground and so hop around. Those that spend as much time on the ground as in trees will both hop and walk. For example, magpies walk when moving slowly on the ground and hop or 'gallop' when moving fast. Birds that spend little time in trees, i.e. the wading birds and sea birds, almost always walk or run. Running or walking is generally faster and more stable then hopping, but for some species hopping is more energy-efficient. Try it for yourself and see what you think.

12. Can you feed garden birds all year round?

Yes, you can. Between the months of April and September it is advisable to put out only seeds. Raw peanuts (not salted, or dry roasted!) should be put out in mesh feeders. Other foods will be too low in energy. The only foods to avoid giving birds at any time are dehydrated items such as desiccated coconut and dried fruit, which may kill birds if eaten in large quantities. During the breeding season birds will take the food you put out only if natural food sources are unavailable, such as during prolonged periods of heavy rain or during unseasonable cold spells.

13. How do birds stay warm in the winter and cool in the summer?

In the short, cold winter days birds that feed only during the day get all their energy to keep warm from what they eat. Heat loss is reduced by puffing up the feathers and trapping air near the skin – the air warms up and acts like insulation or a quilt. Some small birds, such as wrens and tits, also keep warm during cold winter nights by sleeping close together in a communal roost. If, for some reason, they cannot feed for even a day or two, they will not be able to stay warm and will either starve or freeze to death. When birds want to cool down in hot weather they flatten their feathers. Birds do not sweat (perspire) like us. Instead they pant like a dog and also lose heat through their legs.

14. How long do birds live?

A general rule is that the smaller the bird the shorter its life span. For example, 50 percent of all wrens do not survive their first winter. Few live more than two years. Larger birds such as blackbirds or crows will live for five to eight years. Swans and seagulls can live to be over twenty and Manx shearwaters can live to be over thirty years old. Albatrosses, which have been seen in Ireland on less than ten occasions, live a long time, with some reaching seventy years or more.

15. Are birds intelligent?

Birds are often given far more credit for their intelligence than they deserve. Their brains are small and not highly developed (hence the term 'bird brain'), though many have a capacity for learning.

Most birds are probably of similar intelligence, but certain species, because of their close contact with humans, have gained a reputation for being more intelligent than others. The crow family is one example, noted for their perseverance in getting food and escaping from traps. Members of the tit family have been shown to learn to recognise colours by being rewarded with food when they removed the correct coloured stick from a rack. Like crows, they also learned to remove foil tops from glass bottles to get at the milk. Recently there have been reports of crows piercing cardboard milk cartons!

16. Where and when do birds sleep?

A bird sleeping is usually said to be 'at roost' or 'roosting'.

The feeding habits of birds generally dictate where and when they sleep. Some, such as the owls, sleep on their own. They sleep or roost during the day, in a barn, ruin or on a tree, where they will sit motionless, hidden by their camouflaged plumage. The short-eared owl, which comes to Ireland in the winter, hunts in the early morning and late evening and sleeps at night. Seabirds and waterbirds often sleep on their own or in large groups on water away from land, where they are safe from predators. Seagulls roost in very large flocks, some-times as many as 10,000 birds, at regular roost sites, flying there each evening many miles from where they were feeding during the day.

Waders that feed by sense of touch roost in large flocks only at high tide, when the mud and sand is covered up by water. Thus,

sometimes they sleep during the day and sometimes at night. Larger waders do not need to feed as frequently as smaller ones and so will also roost at low tide. Sleeping or roosting in a flock is safer because there are more eyes and ears to sense danger. Most passerines or land birds roost in groups in trees, bushes, or reedbeds at night. A very unusual example of this is the pied wagtail which often roosts in trees in the centre of large towns and cities. There is a theory that birds such as the wagtail get information during the roosting period and follow others in the morning to good feeding areas. The swift sleeps on the wing, high in the sky, gliding on 'autopilot' for up to 150 kilometres each night. During the breeding season most birds roost on or near the nest.

Plumage moult in the gannet, left to right: 1st year, 2nd year, 4th year, adult.

17. Do birds have the same feathers all their life?

Feathers must be strong, light and flexible to do their work. Like mammals shedding old hairs as new ones grow, birds replace old, worn feathers with new ones. Birds have evolved a system for replacing or moulting feathers to ensure that feather function is maintained. Birds in Ireland moult all their feathers at least once a year, usually in the autumn, though some, such as the gulls, also moult their body feathers in the spring. Young birds will usually replace all of their body feathers and some wing feathers in their first autumn, afterwards having a complete moult at that time each year. There are exceptions, such as the young of house sparrows and starlings, which undergo a complete moult of all their feathers.

Moulting can be different for males and females. Like most Irish duck species, the male mallard, for example, moults in June and does it so fast that it is flightless for up to four weeks, while the female moults after the young are independent, usually in July or August. For the mute swan it is the exact opposite: the female becomes flightless two or three weeks after the cygnets have hatched while the male starts moulting only when the female regains her full power of flight.

Some of our migratory birds moult completely before leaving Ireland; others moult partially here and finish the process on arrival at summer or wintering grounds, while a few will wait until the migration flight is over.

The new feathers grow in place of the old ones, pushing them out. This results in gaps, most evident on the tail and wings, until the new feathers have grown completely. Most land birds moult in such a way that they are always able to fly. Look at crows in late June and July and you will see their wings and tails in moult, some birds flying around tailless and with many wing feathers missing.

18. Do we know much about Irish birds?

The documented study of birds in Ireland goes back many centuries. One of the first to make notes on the birdlife of Ireland was Giraldus Cambrensis, a Welsh monk who visited Ireland in 1183 and 1185. While doubt exists about the accuracy of his accounts, they are at least a starting point. Others followed over the next six centuries. It was the beginning of the 19th century that saw an acceleration of published material on Irish birds. Books like *The Natural History of Ireland Vols 1-3* by William Thompson (1859-61) and a series of papers like 'American Bird-visitors to Ireland at Home' (1893-94) by the much-travelled W.E. Praeger were the fore-runners of the major work at the turn of the century *The Birds of Ireland* by Ussher and Warren. Bird study continued to accelerate and in 1954 a comprehensive account of Irish birds entitled *The Birds of Ireland* was published by Kennedy, Ruttledge and Scroope.

Many studies on individual species have revealed new information on a wide range of birds found in Ireland, including work in the early part of this century on robins and whitethroats by J.P. Burkitt and, more recently, work on dippers by Ken Perry and on mute swans by Richard Collins and Dr. John O'Halloran.

Ringing birds, which involves the placing of a very light, individually marked metal ring on a bird's leg by a qualified ringer (licensed by the OPW or DOE), has expanded our knowledge considerably, especially in the areas of migration, bird behaviour and biology. There are ninety qualified bird-ringers in Ireland involved in a broad range of bird studies.

Longterm studies at bird observatories on Copeland Island, County Down, Great Saltee Island, County Wexford, and Cape Clear Island, County Cork, continue to produce much valuable information.

Work on the distribution of both breeding birds and wintering birds in Ireland in the last thirty years has resulted in three joint publications by the IWC and the British Trust for Ornithology (BTO). Two books on breeding birds and one on wintering birds were the result of co-ordinated surveys involving thousands of hours of work by both amateur and professional birdwatchers over three-year periods giving us the clearest and most comprehensive picture to date of the distribution and population of Irish birds.

Since 1989, the IWC has been running the Winter Garden Bird Feeding survey, in which members of the organisation monitor birds coming to feed on food put out for them during December, January and February. This is a long-term study designed to monitor the fortunes of Ireland's common species.

Journals such as *Irish Birds*, published annually by the IWC, and the *Irish Naturalists Journal* feature the results of studies on Irish birds today. Our knowledge of Irish birds continues to grow and, through organisations such as the IWC and RSPB, as well as through third-level education establishments and government bodies, much more will be added to the large body of work that already exists.

19. Why do some birds of the same species have different plumage?

There are a number of reasons for this. One is that in species where the female incubates the eggs, dull colours act to camouflage the birds from predators. The mallard is one example where the male is very brightly-coloured and the female is brown and so is very difficult to see when she is sitting on her nest. Another reason involves courtship. The male with the brightest plumage – and, therefore, probably the healthiest – will often be chosen by the female. It has been shown that male swallows with very long outer tail feathers are more successful at finding a mate than swallows with shorter ones. The males of some species, such as the finches and buntings, get their colourful breeding plumage by the gradual wearing down of dull-coloured feather tips during the winter, revealing the brighter colours below. With the red-necked phalarope, which is a small wading bird, roles are reversed and it is the female which is the most colourful. After she lays her eggs, it is the duller-coloured male which incubates them alone until they hatch. The female flies off immediately to find another mate!

20. How many different types of bird have been seen in Ireland?

Some 418 different species of wild bird have been seen in Ireland, up to July 1994. Many are common, either as resident species or as summer or winter visitors. Some are scarce, occurring regularly but only in small numbers. The remainder are rare, occurring only once or twice a year. Some species on the Irish list have not been seen in over a hundred years, though new species are being added almost every year.

Most birdwatchers keep a list of the species they have seen. Those for whom their list is the main motivation for birdwatching are usually called 'twitchers', because it is said that when they see a new species they twitch with excitement. They will travel the length and breadth of the island in search of new species. There is even a special telephone line operating 24 hours a day, 365 days a year, which will give updated information on all the rare-bird news in Ireland. The number is: 1550-111-700 (Republic only) and 0247-467408 for Northern Ireland (prefix 08- from the Republic). In recent years one or two very rare birds have attracted over 300 twitchers, some travelling from Britain, and not all lucky enough to see the bird. The top twitchers in Ireland have seen over 300 species.

Birdwatch racing, in which teams of four try to see or hear as many bird species as possible in a twenty-four hour period, is increasing in popularity and has shown that it is possible to see over 120 species in Ireland on a good day.

Birds and Conservation

WHY CONSERVE BIRDS?

There are many reasons why we should conserve bird life. Firstly, birds play a very important part in the web of life on our planet. They provide us with food, beauty and inspiration. Within the food chain, they play a vital role, for example in controlling 'pest' insects or clearing carrion. Without birds our lives overall would be much duller.

There are many ways in which you can help to conserve our birds, which are, after all, a part of our natural heritage. We have a responsibility to future generations to protect these natural wonders which are so often taken for granted when they are common and which can become irretrievably lost so easily.

Through bird conservation we will also be able to retain our countryside's wild habitats, because, as already stated, birds do not live in isolation. Therefore, by conserving birds we will also have to conserve and take care of the places where they live, which is almost every type of habitat you can think of, from the ocean to the mountains.

In modern society money plays a part in everything, and nature is no exception. With so many demands on our planet, it is unrealistic to expect people to starve in order to protect some rare or exotic birds or for people to be deprived of their livelihoods to preserve an important habitat. However, with a little thought and a lot of understanding and compromise, it is possible for wildlife and 'development' to co-exist.

BIRDS AND THE LAW

Governments have come to realise that we need laws to avoid uncontrolled destruction of our wild creatures and their habitats.

In the Republic of Ireland, birds are protected by the 1976 Wildlife Act and in Northern Ireland by the 1985 Wildlife Order. These laws are similar in both parts of the island and are constantly updated as circumstances for our birds and other wildlife continue to change. At present, all birds are protected by law, but for certain species 'seasons' are declared in which they can be killed. For example, all duck species can be shot between 1 September and 31 January. Other 'game' species with a hunting season include snipe, pheasant and grouse. All goose species are fully protected. Some species such as crows (excluding chough and raven) and gulls are sometimes called 'vermin' and can be shot all year round. Bullfinches can be killed in orchards only if crop damage can be proven. Birds which form large flocks, such as lapwings and starlings, can be killed under licence if they are considered a threat to air traffic. In severe winter weather, where many birds may become very weak through cold and starvation, hunting may be stopped or suspended by ministerial order.

The trapping of all wild birds is illegal. The only exceptions are when a licence is given to qualified bird-ringers for the purpose of studying birds which are released unharmed, and for pest control, as in the case of pigeons in food warehouses etc.

Not very long ago the trapping of finches was a relatively common practice with many houses having a caged linnet or goldfinch. Despite the fact that the majority of people now regard this as cruel and unnecessary, illegal trapping still continues. It is not illegal to have 'wild' bird species reared from captive stock.

One of the main functions of the IWC and the RSPB is to ensure that the laws relating to wild birds are enforced and, on occasion, co-operate with the authorities in taking legal action against those who break these laws. Through the monitoring of bird populations they will also make recommendations for changes in the law if it is thought to be inadequate.

HOW CAN WE HELP CONSERVE BIRDS?

At local level

Like many other things, bird conservation begins at home. There are many ways on the local level you can help birds to survive.

1. If you have a garden, see page 89 for details on how you can make it more 'bird-friendly'.

2. The plastic rings holding packs of beer or soft drink cans together can get caught around birds' necks and result in their suffering a long, slow, agonising death. Always cut up these plastic rings before throwing them in the bin and if you come across them bring them home or tear them up on the spot.

3. When using a can opener always take the top of the tin completely off. Many birds lose their legs on the razor-sharp edge of the lid. It is very upsetting to see a bird with its leg caught in this lethal trap.

4. Discarded fishing line is another lethal trap for birds, so always cut the line up into small pieces before disposing of it in a waste bin. Also try to avoid using lead weights. Safe substitutes are available. Lost lead can find its way into mute swans and other wildfowl and poison them.

5. Write to your local authority asking it to ensure that all hedge-cutting is carried out before the breeding season for hedgerow birds.

6. If you live in the country why not plant some trees? And if you do not live on a farm, why not ask a friendly farmer if you could plant a small corner of unused ground, no matter how small, with some native trees and shrubs, most of which can be grown easily from seed. Remember that most of the deciduous wood in Ireland today was planted over a hundred years ago by people who knew that they would not live to see its true beauty, and we can be thankful for their vision. In today's world of instant everything, the idea of starting something that you will never see finished sounds crazy, but we must not let this put us off.

7. Look around your area and identify small ponds, stands of trees or any 'wild' areas (unfortunately referred to by some as 'wasteland'). If possible, get a map and mark them in and write a short letter to your local authority, outlining the importance of these areas for wildlife. Ask them to keep your submission on file for future reviews of their development plan for your area. Local authorities often welcome such information as it makes them aware of your concern for these sites. They might not seem very important at

present but, as other areas are destroyed, their value will increase greatly with time.

The golden rule in local conservation is never to wait until a site comes under threat to try to save it, as this may be too late. How often do we walk a regular path and one day find some small pond or group of trees that we used to admire obliterated by a high-tech, super-efficient demolition machine? It is too late by then to protest. Don't wait for someone else to protect your environment, because they probably won't.

Any arguments for saving a wildlife area should always be backed by scientific data. Contact the IWC or RSPB and ask their advice. The area in which you are interested may have been included in a survey at some time in the past and any information on its wildlife value would strengthen your case. Unfortunately in this age of budgets and cash-strapped local authorities, arguments based solely on emotion will rarely save 'your' site.

At national level

Bird conservation at national level is similar to that at local level but on a larger scale. You are dealing with many interested parties, all vying for the same piece of land for totally different purposes. The best way to contribute to national bird and wildlife conservation is to join the IWC in the Republic or the RSPB in Northern Ireland. The larger the membership of such organisations the more they will be listened to by politicians who, in turn, can influence government policies in relation to conservation.

You can also write to your local representatives asking their views on conservation.

In 1993 the IWC, with the help of RSPB Northern Ireland and the co-operation of the OPW and the DOE, produced 'Conservation Strategy for Birds in Ireland', an analysis of species and habitats most requiring protection. This identified 92 species of conservation value in terms of international importance, and in terms of declining, local or rare status. Ireland's most threatened habitats and breeding species identified in this document are listed below. National support for the action plans which have been produced to save these species and habitats is essential.

IRELAND'S MOST THREATENED SPECIES AND HABITATS

BREEDING SPECIES	HABITAT
common scoter	lowland wet grassland
hen harrier	machair (sandy coastal lowlands)
red grouse	bogs
grey partridge	fens
quail	waterside vegetation
corncrake	non-intensive grassland
golden plover	inter-tidal flats
lapwing	salt marsh
roseate tern	coastal lagoons
barn owl	
nightjar	
corn bunting	

At international level

Birds are the best example of the need for a global approach to wildlife conservation. Ireland plays host to hundreds of thousands of birds which spend part of their year in another country, often very far away and necessitating a flight that will take them across many countries. For example, the swallow, which comes to Ireland each summer to raise its young, undertakes a very hazardous journey to reach here. Apart from having to survive the winter months south of the Sahara, it will, when it starts its migration in spring, first have to endure the harsh conditions over the Sahara desert. If it succeeds, it will face a terrifying trip over the Mediterranean where (spring and autumn combined) over 9,000,000 (this is *not* a misprint) migratory birds are killed by hunters each year. Similarly, geese that are protected in Ireland are shot in other countries on their way south to winter here each year. If we want birds such as the swallow to return to us each summer, it is vital that international cooperation between governments is encouraged. Many international treaties already exist to protect birds, such as the European Communities Directive on the Conservation of Wild Birds and the Council of Europe Convention on the Conservation of European Wildlife and Natural Habitats (also known as the Berne Convention). Birdlife International (of which the IWC is the representative in the Republic and the RSPB in Northern Ireland) is the organisation

dedicatedtotheconservationofwildbirdsthroughouttheworld.
It promotes conservation plans which include local initiatives,
such as eco-tourism, to protect globally-endangered bird species. By joining the IWC or the RSPB you will be supporting bird
conservation at an international level.

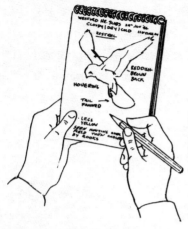

Birdwatching – Getting Started

THE NOTEBOOK

The most important book in birdwatching is your notebook. This is used to write down what you have seen, where and when you saw it, and anything you feel is important to keep as a record. It is also used to take descriptions of birds you cannot readily identify. Without your notebook, by the time you look at an identification guide, blue may become green, grey may turn to black, streaking disappear, and size and shape become distorted beyond belief. You may end up convincing yourself that the bird you spotted is the same as the first bird you come across in the book which looks vaguely like it, passing over 'minor' details such as that it has never been seen before in Ireland, is a flightless species found only on remote islands in the Pacific or that there are three very similar species far more common than this one.

With a little practice, you can record a large amount of information about a bird in a short space of time by using

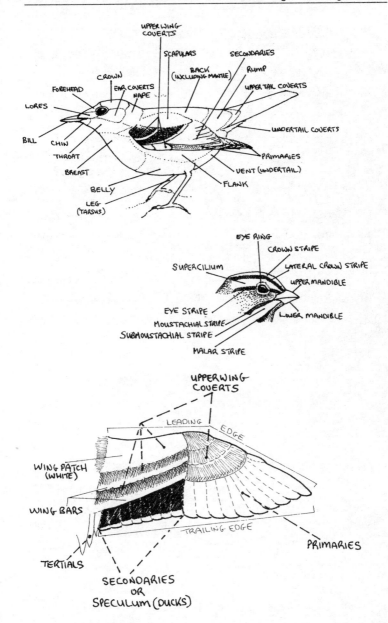

drawings or sketches. You do not need a degree in art. In fact, you do not need to be able to draw well at all. (Most people can draw better than they imagine!) If you wanted to give someone directions you would preferably draw a map rather than have them remember it all in their head. When identifying birds it is the same thing – think of your humble sketch as a map rather than a work of art. Things to look at when taking notes are as follows:

SIZE

Birds are rarely found on their own. There are nearly always other birds close by. If there is a bird you know nearby compare it with your mystery bird and note down its size, i.e. twice the size of a robin or smaller than a crow or bigger than a seagull. Try to do this without looking through binoculars or telescopes as these can sometimes distort size.

SHAPE

Bill shapes: 1. insect eater, 2. seed eater, 3. meat eater, 4. fish eater

When identifying a bird, judging its shape is very important. A bird's shape is determined by the place where it usually lives. The essential parts of a bird to look at are the bill, legs, wings and tail. Is the bill long and thin like a curlew or short and thick like a finch? Are the legs short or long, thin or fat? Are the wings long and narrow like a swift or broad and short like a pheasant?

Is the tail long like a magpie or short like a herring gull? It is also very useful to note the shape of the end of a bird's tail – is it square, rounded, wedge shaped or notched?

PATTERNS

TAIL PATTERNS (left to right): plain, plain, black tail band, white outer tail feathers, plain.
TAIL SHAPES (left to right): forked, notched, square-ended, round-ended, wedge-ended.

The variety of patterns, stripes, lines, patches, bars, spots, etc. on birds is almost infinite. Recording the most striking patterns is important. Firstly, note the wing patterns. Are there any patches, stripes or wing bars? Is the tail all one colour? Look carefully. Many birds such as finches and buntings have pale outer tail feathers. The tails of gulls might have a dark band on the end. The back might be plain or striped, sometimes very subtly. The underside might be plain, streaked, spotted, or a combination of all three! Head patterns on birds can be very complex. The rook has a plain head pattern but the ringed plover has a very complicated one. Record any features that stand out and try to get to know the different parts of a bird from studying the diagrams in this book. Don't worry if you can remember only some of the parts. Your knowledge will improve with practice.

COLOUR

One area of bird identification that can cause great difficulty is the description of the colours of birds. For instance, rooks are not actually black but a beautiful dark iridescent blue. Light conditions and wear of the feathers alter colour. Whether the feathers are wet or dry will also affect their colour. All these things must be borne in mind when describing the colours on your mystery bird. Try to refer to colours of birds you already know, e.g. robin red, blue tit blue etc. It is not always enough to say that the bird was brown. You should always try to be more exact. For instance, it might have been grey-brown, which means that is was mainly brown with a hint of grey, or red-brown, which is also mainly brown but with a hint of red. Both of these colours are brown, but look completely different from each other. Some birds can be partly or completely albino, most noticeable on birds with dark plumage (see page 41). These white feathers might make it hard to identify a bird which would otherwise be easy to categorise. Finally, don't forget to record the colour of the bird's legs, bill and eyes, but beware – wet or dry mud or earth on bill and legs will often hide the real colour.

CALL AND SONG

Bird calls and songs have been the inspiration for many poets, such as Shakespeare, Hardy and Clarke, and composers such as Mahler, Sibelius, Ravel, and many traditional Irish musicians. But try as they may, even these experts of sound have struggled in vain to record accurately what birds sound like.

What is the difference between a call and a song? A call is

usually very short and not at all musical and is the sound a bird makes when it wants to tell others of its own kind where it is. An example is the call of a finch as the flock flies over a field, or that of long-tailed tits moving along a hedgerow. This keeps the flock together and raises the  alarm for other members of the flock when danger is near. The song, however, is usually very musical and is used primarily to tell other birds of its own kind to keep out of its territory and also to attract a mate. As a general rule the duller the colour of the bird the more musical is its song.

If you do not have a tape-recorder handy to record the song or call of your mystery bird then write down what it sounded like. A song 'graph' might help, to show where the notes went up or down and where there were pauses between notes. People have used words and phrases to remind them of a bird's song. For example a yellowhammer 'says' something like 'a little bit of bread and no cheese'. Separating the calls of the collared dove and woodpigeon is easy if you remember that collared doves seem to say *Can yoouuu coo ... can yoouuu coo ...*, while the similar-sounding woodpigeon 'says' *Take two, John, take two.*

HABITS

Finally, it is important not only to note a physical description of the bird but also what it was doing and where it was seen. Was it wagging its tail all the time? Was it always on the ground or in bushes? Was its flight fast and straight like a wren or slow and undulating like a finch? Did it fly close to the ground or high in the air? What was the habitat where you saw the bird, i.e. a beach, up a mountain, on or near water? Did it stand up straight or horizontally? Did it stay out in the open or did it hide in long grass or deep in a bush most of the time? Was it calling all the time? Was it singing out in the open or out of sight? All these things are very important

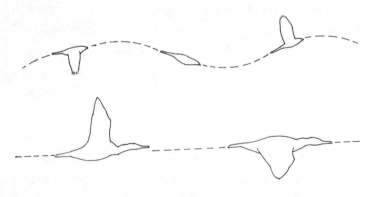

Flight patterns

because, while there are exceptions to every rule, birds generally like certain habitats and have habits peculiar to themselves.

Learning to record what you see and hear will improve with practice. The value of your records will also increase with time, both personally and in helping to monitor the fortunes of birds and helping in their conservation.

THINGS TO DO

1. Find some photographs of birds and write a description of them. Compare your description with that in this or another bird book.
2. Practise naming the different bird parts, shapes and patterns by covering over the names in the illustrations.

EQUIPMENT

BINOCULARS

 In every hobby, even if you have no spare cash, there is always something 'else' that you will feel you need. A pair of binoculars is definitely the second item to get after a notebook. While many species are easily identifiable without optical aids, the more interested you become the more apparent it will be that you really must get that little bit closer to the birds you see. A pair of binoculars is what you need. If you go to a shop selling optical equipment, you will be dazzled and confused by the jargon and the array of binoculars available. Before you even think of buying, take the following advice. On the binoculars you will usually find two numbers near the eye-pieces, e.g. 10 x 50. These two numbers will tell you most of the information you need to know. The first number refers to the magnification of the binoculars, i.e. ten times. The second number refers to the diameter in millimetres of the objective lenses, the ones furthest from your eyes. The bigger this number the more light

gets through to your eye. For general use 7x30, 8x30 or 8x40 binoculars are ideal, fairly powerful but light and compact. Holding binoculars steady up to your eyes for more than a few moments can be very tiring and on a cold January afternoon the shake from your hands might lead you to believe that you are experiencing Ireland's strongest earthquake! The relatively new compact binoculars, while being small enough to fit into a coat pocket, have a small objective lens and so do not let in much light and will have a small field of view. You can spend anything from £30 to £800 on your binoculars. It is advisable to start with a pair that are inexpensive, as binoculars over £200 are really for the specialists. Always remember that having the most up-to-date equipment will not automatically make you a better bird-watcher. In camera shops that sell second-hand equipment, good cheap binoculars can often be found. Never buy a pair of binoculars without looking through them first and don't be too quick to buy. After all, if the binoculars are not comfortable to your eyes they may end up damaging your eyesight.

ADJUSTING BINOCULARS BEFORE USE

Eyesight varies from person to person and often one eye is better than the other. Adjusting binoculars before using them is very important. Using the central focusing wheel, focus on something with sharp contrast, such as a sign-post or poster, fifteen or twenty metres away, and do not worry if the image is not very sharp. Then put a piece of paper or thin cardboard over the adjustable eyepiece and refocus on the sign-post or poster. Then block the fixed eyepiece and focus with the adjustable eyepiece until the image is sharp. The binoculars are now adjusted to suit your eyes. Do not block your eye with your hand when adjusting the binoculars because the pressure of the hand on the closed eye can temporarily impair vision and so defeat the purpose of the exercise. Often there are numbers on the adjustable eyepiece, so you can remember the setting that suits you.

If you cannot afford to buy a pair of binoculars, someone might have a broken pair and if the side with the adjustable eyepiece is undamaged it could be used as a monocular.

Remember the following tips when choosing a pair of binoculars:

1. Never buy the first pair of binoculars you look at. You will be hoping to get long use from them and it is wise to look around at the large selection now available.

2. Before looking through the binoculars, check them for scratches on the glass or bumps on the metal and make sure that the central focusing wheel moves freely.

3. Look through the opposite end of the binoculars for damage or dust inside. (This applies to telescopes also.)

4. There should be a coating on the lenses, usually blue but sometimes green or yellow.

5. Adjust the focusing as explained above.

6. Check for any colour difference between the objects you are looking at and what you see through the binoculars.

7. Some binoculars can focus closer than others. The closer they can focus the better.

8. Check for the amount of blurring (if any) at the edges of the image in view.

9. The weight of the binoculars is very important. Holding binoculars up to your eyes for even a few minutes can be quite tiring. Make sure you are comfortable with them.

THINGS TO DO

If you get a pair of binoculars, practise with them before starting on a birdwatching expedition. Ask someone to call out objects at different distances and heights and try to find and focus on them as quickly as possible. Many people find locating a bird with binoculars quite difficult at first.

TELESCOPES

Telescopes are especially useful if you want to watch birds at sea or on an estuary or lake, where they can be quite a distance away. A good telescope will cost you over £80 and usually as much as £200 to £300. Do not buy a telescope for looking at the stars (usually white or red in colour). These are too powerful and awkward to use and give a dull image when used in daylight. The best one to get should be 20x60, 30x60 or 25x70 and, above all, should suit yourself.

The IWC 'Wings' shop at Longford Place, Monkstown, Co. Dublin (Tel: 01-280-4322) stocks a large range of binoculars, telescopes and accessories to suit all pockets and can offer expert advice. All profit from sales is used to help bird conservation in Ireland.

CAMERAS

To take good photographs of birds requires, above all, plenty of patience. Unlike buildings or people, birds have a strange habit of flying away, never to be seen again, just when you have got close enough to take a good photograph. Instamatic cameras are generally no good because you cannot get close enough, and since birds can move very fast the image will be blurred.

You will need a 35mm camera with interchangeable lenses. Generally, the bigger the lens the larger the magnification (and the more awkward to use). A lens of between 300mm and 500mm is the best but can be very expensive.

Getting to know the birds you want to photograph will help you get closer without disturbing them. A hide, while cumbersome to carry about, once set up will allow you to get very close pictures without a very powerful lens. Most of the world's top photographers take their best photos from hides. Stalking birds is also a very rewarding way to take good photographs, though the pain factor does increase enormously. Try crawling on one hand and two knees across even the smoothest of lawns while staying perfectly quiet. If you found that no trouble, try crawling across a rocky beach or through nettle- and bramble-infested undergrowth. A relatively easy way to get good pictures of birds is to take them coming to feeders or bird tables in the winter. With a tripod and an extension lead for the shutter release you can get close pictures with even a 50mm lens. You can cheat a little by placing a twig sticking out of the feeder or bird table that birds will use as a perch. If you are careful to avoid including the feeder or table in the frame, the bird will look as if it is in a 'natural' environment.

VIDEO CAMERAS

Once an expensive luxury, the video camera is now almost as cheap as a 35mm camera. Most come with powerful zoom lenses and can be used like the 35mm cameras. The main advantage is that the moving image of a bird you have filmed can help you to learn to identify it. The moving picture gives you a better impression of the bird, not only capturing its colour and shape, but also its sound, habits and jizz. Another advantage is that you can reuse the video tape so you do not end up with hundreds, if not thousands, of out-of-focus, over-exposed photos of your feet, the sky or part of a very interesting bush. Focusing is automatic and you can also instantly see the results of your work. You can set up the video camera at, say, a bird's regular perch, start filming, walk away to a safe distance and wait for the bird to return.

The disadvantages are that batteries must be recharged, are expensive to buy and you will need a lot for a morning's filming. The image you see when filming is black-and-white so trying to film a small bird, in bushes for example, is almost impossible. To get good quality pictures on video you will have to pay a lot of money for your camera (over £1,000). Also, while the ability to use the same tape over and over again sounds economical, in practice most people do not reuse them and you will end up with a mountain of tapes. Video cameras are less robust than 35mm cameras, which in some Irish weather conditions will be a problem.

Finally remember that to get good quality images on either camera or video requires years of hard work. Not only do you have to be very familiar with your instrument, but you must also know the birds you are trying to capture on film. Do not be too disappointed if your first efforts are not as good as they looked through the view-finder.

OPTICAL ACCESSORIES

There are thousands of accessories to be got for your optical equipment and it would take too long to cover them all here. However, a tripod will be invaluable if you get a tele-scope, camera, or video camera, allowing you to get steadier images and not be limited to the nearest wall, rock or fence post. It is possible also to get an attachment for a tri-pod to take a pair of binoculars. This can be very handy as shake is eliminated and it frees the hands for note-taking etc. Monopods, often seen being used by professional photographers at sports events, are less cumber-some than tripods though not as steady.

CARE FOR OPTICAL AIDS

Some birdwatchers can go through half-a-dozen pairs of binoculars and two or three cameras and telescopes during their lifetime. One of the first rules in birdwatching is to leave the cases and covers of binoculars, telescopes or cameras at home. This is because you have to be always ready for that split-second chance of seeing something new or unusual. By the time the case is removed the bird is gone. Therefore, it is very important to remember a few simple tips to increase the lifespan of your prize possession.

1. Buy or make a rain/dust-guard which will cover both eyepieces at the same time and which can be attached to the strap.
2. Before attempting to clean the glass on binoculars, first remove any grit or sand from inside the rims with a dry artist's paint-brush, or a camera air-brush. Grit and sand will scratch the glass.
3. Clean the lenses on binoculars, telescopes and cameras only with a clean, dry soft material. Tissues leave fibres on the glass.
4. Do not rub the lenses too hard as this will eventually remove the special optical coating.
5. If you get seawater on your optical equipment, wipe it down with a warm, slightly damp cloth and leave it in a warm place to dry.
6. Resist the temptation to dismantle binoculars or telescopes. This usually signals the beginning of the end of your optical equipment. Optical repairs specialists advertise in bird and photographic magazines.

When using any optical aid it is important to remember not to disturb birds, especially if they have young. You should avoid trying to take pictures of nesting birds as you might cause the parents to desert. For rare species it is illegal to film at the nest without a permit (Northern Ireland only at present). Also remember there might be other people watching the bird you are trying to photograph or film, so be considerate and ask their permission before trying to get a little closer.

Finally, respect people's privacy and private property. Restrain yourself from using any optical equipment on crowded beaches, in town gardens or where there might be houses in the background. Remember, people might not realise that you are interested only in the bird.

CLOTHING

It is obvious that you should conceal yourself as much as possible when birdwatching. Generally speaking, however, there is no need to go to too much trouble. The main thing is to avoid bright colours, extreme examples being almost luminous orange, green or red jackets. While green clothing is desirable, dark blue or brown is just as effective.

If you are trying to get really close to birds then any clothes that rustle, such as PVC-type rainwear, should be avoided. Finally, even during the summer months it can be cold and, if you are birdwatching on the coast or on high ground, gloves and extra warm clothing should be brought, just in case! Many a good day's birdwatching has been ruined by inadequate clothing.

IDENTIFICATION GUIDES

The best way of judging if a bird book is good for identification purposes is to look at the paintings of the birds you already know. If they look true to life then you can be fairly sure that the unfamiliar birds are well-illustrated. Do not get the biggest book available because, even though it might have brilliant text and illustrations, it will most likely contain many rare birds and ones not found in Ireland at all. You will more than likely wrongly identify birds you have seen because there are so many birds in such books that look alike but are found thousands of miles apart.

Bird identification guides with photographs instead of illustrations should really be bought only in addition to a standard, illustrated guide. Some of the photographs in these guides will not show all the important features of the birds and some will not show the colours well. If you are unable to afford a book on bird identification, go to the library and you should find one there.

One of the biggest mistakes you can make when beginning birdwatching is to take a bird book out with you when trying to identify an unfamiliar bird. Firstly the bird will almost definitely fly away before you open the book – and you will end up spending more time looking through the book and less time looking at the bird and will probably mis-identify it in the end.

Reference books should be looked at only after the bird has gone and preferably after you have taken note of the main features of the bird.

ATTRACTING BIRDS

Because they are able to fly, birds can be seen almost anywhere on the planet. Therefore, to start birdwatching you need go no further than the nearest window. Once you can see the sky and even a small piece of ground outside you are in business. You do not have to have a garden or live in the country, though either would be a bonus. Over the course of a year you could easily identify 20 to 25 species, and in some circumstances up to 40 species without leaving your room.

You can increase your chances of seeing birds in many ways. Putting out food and water for birds is probably the easiest and most rewarding way of attracting birds and can be done without costing you a small fortune. The following list of suggestions is not exhaustive. Do not hesitate to try out your own variations.

FOOD

When feeding birds, it is important that the feeding area is clean and that food is not allowed to get mouldy. Birds, like all living creatures, are prone to disease and if the feeding area is not kept clean you might unintentionally kill your little visitors.

All types of seeds and nuts can be used. If you intend to feed birds all winter, buying in small quantities is uneconomical. You will find that during hard weather and in the months of January and February the seed and nuts you put out will disappear at a phenomenal rate, so it is wise to buy in bulk. Club together with friends. On average, 12kg of peanuts and 12kg of mixed bird seed will last from October to March or April.

It is very important to ensure that the peanuts you buy are 'bird quality', because inferior peanuts often have a mould growing on them which is lethal to birds. Store your seed and peanuts in dry, air-tight containers. Well-washed old plastic paint containers are ideal.

Never put out whole peanuts, for two good reasons. Firstly, they will disappear as fast as you can put them out. Many species hoard peanuts if they can be removed in one piece – one group of coal tits removed a quarter of a kilogram of peanuts in one hour! If you continued this practice you would be bankrupt by the end of the winter. The other reason is that, during the breeding season, birds which cannot find a natural food supply may be tempted to feed their young whole nuts, causing the young birds to choke.

Other recommended foods include apples, porridge oats, bread and other kitchen scraps. Apples are particularly good for members of the thrush family. Porridge oats, bread and other kitchen scraps are best put out mixed with melted suet or solid vegetable oil to form a cake. This stops the food from blowing all over the place and provides a protective coating which helps it last longer. The fat also provides extra energy for the birds. A general guide is to mix three parts food with one part fat/solid vegetable oil. Suitable containers include half a coconut shell, an empty yoghurt container or an empty milk carton cut in half.

If you want to be really adventurous, you can put out the carcass of the Sunday roast chicken or the Christmas turkey, or indeed any cooked meat bones. The only drawback is that it might be a little disturbing for visitors looking out your window and seeing a hungry great tit disappear into the rib cage of yesterday's dinner!

Remember that, whatever amount of food you put out, you should not overdo it. The birds can take only so much and the excess will either rot or attract undesirables such as rats. The beauty of feeding birds outside your window is that you have the company and entertainment of these beautiful creatures almost all year round without the responsibility of pets. Remember, if you stop feeding 'your' birds, they will soon find someone else and will not spend days sitting on your window-sill like a cat or a dog demanding to be fed.

Now that you have an idea of what food to put out for birds the next thing to know is where to put the food. There is an ever-increasing array of bird feeders appearing on the market and if you are thinking of buying one be very careful. Many of the commercially available feeders look nice but are totally impractical. The best ones to get are the simplest ones.

PEANUT FEEDERS

For peanuts, wire mesh (4mm) feeders are the best. They are cheap, long-lasting and prevent the birds from extracting whole nuts. One design even has a large plastic dish at the bottom. This is tidier and reduces the amount of broken peanuts ending up on the ground. There is a large selection of good designs available. The main advantages of the mesh feeders is that they are clean and neat and can be hung or mounted almost anywhere. Be sure that the lid on the feeder cannot easily pop off, as greedy birds can get trapped inside half-empty cylindrical mesh feeders. Always use wire or very strong string to hang out your feeder. Crows have been known to fly off with them (and the neighbours' children are usually suspected!). A second piece of wire or string tied near the bottom will stop crows from up-ending the contents onto the ground. In some areas grey squirrels are also a problem. Squirrel-proof feeders are available though some are not 100 percent successful. The main disadvantage of putting out a peanut feeder is that, once birds have found the feeder, you will be under enormous pressure to get more.

SEED DISPENSERS

Apart from striped sunflower seeds, most seeds are unsuitable for the mesh feeders. They are too small and will slip through the mesh. In the wind they come out like salt out of a salt cellar. If you mix the seed with suet or vegetable fat (seed cake), then the seed can be put on an old dish or small lid. The seed can

SEED
HOPPER.

also be put in a half co-
conut or a shallow tin.

If you prefer to put out
seed dry, the best way
is to use a seed hopper,
which is usually a wedge- or
cone-shaped container with a
narrow opening at the bottom onto
a dish or bird table. They are usually not very good if suspended, as seed
will be scattered everywhere on windy days. Also if the seed gets
wet it may germinate, swell up, and block the opening. It is very
important to use seed hoppers in sheltered locations. A large
'roof' is essential to help keep the seed dry.

Recently, American-style seed dispensers have appeared on
the market here which basically consist of a clear perspex or
plastic cylinder with a varying number of recessed feeding-holes.
Some people have had great success with this type of feeder
while others have been very disappointed. Persistence usually
pays off as the birds visiting you may take up to a month to learn
how to get food from this type of dispenser.

BIRD TABLES

Without doubt bird tables are by far the best place to put your
food for the birds. They can be bought at garden centres and
department stores. The design and quality vary enormously and
there are a few essential points to remember when buying or
making a bird table.

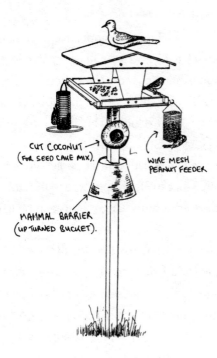

CUT COCONUT →
(FOR SEED CAKE MIX).

WIRE MESH
PEANUT FEEDER

MAMMAL BARRIER
(UP TURNED BUCKET).

The ideal bird table.

1. Do not be attracted to the most ornate table available. While it might look great in the garden it may be impractical, providing easy access for cats.

2. Think simple and strong. Ideally, the table should have a roof. This gives shelter for the food and birds and also deters larger birds and makes life very difficult for cats.

3. Always make sure there is a lip around the edge of the table and a gap at each corner for drainage. Otherwise you will end up with a swimming pool not a feeding table.

BUiLDING A BIRD TABLE

If you are building a table it does not have to be of professional standard and once the wood is weather-proofed each year there should be no other maintenance. There should be approximately a four-inch gap between the roof and the table. This allows most birds to get food while excluding very large birds such as crows. If you already have a table and the gap is too big, coat-hanger wire can be used to exclude these larger visitors. two-inch-square chicken wire can also be put around the table if you want to keep out the bigger birds. Larger birds can be fed separately if you wish.

Put a few nails or hooks on the side of the table for hanging a peanut feeder or a half-coconut, seedcake or some fruit. An empty two-litre milk container or other plastic container, with the rim removed, firmly placed 30 centimetres below the table, making sure it cannot be tilted, will stop most animals from gaining access to a free meal.

When you have bought or built your bird table, it is very important to site it carefully. Never put the table too near a hedge, wall or bushes. It will quickly become the local take-away for the cats in the neighbourhood. Place it at least six feet from these to allow the birds to see danger coming.

Do not put the table down at the end of the garden. The birds will still come but you will be lucky to identify any of them.

Site the table as near to the house or viewing area as possible. You need only avoid putting it where a lot of people are likely to be coming and going. The birds will quickly become accus-

Bird table to avoid!

tomed to people inside the house and ignore you after a while, flying away only if you open a window or door or someone appears outside. If you have dogs or cats and live in a two-storey house, you can always hang peanut feeders off an upstairs window.

Bird tables are best placed on a pole in the ground as they can easily be blown over in the wind. The table should be at least five feet off the ground and preferably at eye level in relation to your viewing position. A table on a stand needs to be in a sheltered spot and can be anchored in the ground by metal

83

brackets made up from 10mm metal rods or by using bricks or concrete blocks on a hard surface area. Wherever you put it, it is wise to ensure that it can be moved. During the summer months it might get in the way or be damaged when children are using the garden. This is also convenient for maintenance.

WATER

Water is very important for birds, especially during the winter. A small bird-bath will attract a surprisingly large range of birds. Water can be put out in a wide variety of containers, but all should be shallow (not more than four inches at the deepest). Anything from a biscuit-tin lid to a garden pond will do. An old dustbin lid is ideal. If the bottom of a broken plastic dustbin or a large plastic container (minimum 50 centimetres diameter) is removed, this will also make a fine bird-bath. When you are

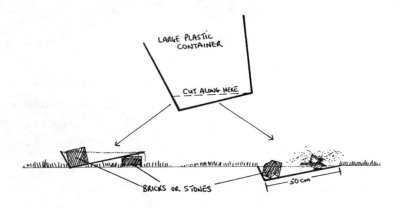

Making a simple bird bath.

cutting the end off the dustbin or any other plastic container do not cut it straight across but at an angle thus providing a sloping bottom to allow birds to walk in to whatever depth suits them best. Dig a shallow hole in the garden to accommodate the bird-bath. If you are not putting it in the ground put a stone or brick under the shallow end. You will also need to put a stone in the deep end of the bird-bath to stop it from being blown away in a gust of wind. Put the bird-bath in the open, like the bird table, to avoid ambushes by cats. Replace the water if it starts looking murky or filled with leaves. In frosty weather, break the ice if you have a pond or empty and refill the container early in the morning. Do not use hot or warm water as this may kill the birds quicker than the cold.

TOP TEN SPECIES VISITING IRISH BIRD FEEDERS*

RURAL	SUBURBAN/URBAN
1. robin	1. robin
2. blue tit	2. blue tit
3. blackbird	3. blackbird
4. chaffinch	4. chaffinch
5. great tit	5. great tit
6. coal tit	6. house sparrow
7. greenfinch	7. greenfinch
8. magpie[+]	8. starling
9. song thrush[+]	9. coal tit
10. dunnock	10. dunnock

[+] *These species were recorded even if they did not take food.*

OTHER SPECIES RECORDED VISITING IRISH GARDENS*

barn owl

blackcap

black-headed gull

brambling

bullfinch

chiffchaff

collared dove

common gull

feral pigeon

fieldfare

goldcrest

goldfinch

grey heron

grey wagtail

herring gull

hooded crow

jackdaw

jay

kestrel

linnet

long-eared owl

long-tailed tit

meadow pipit

mistle thrush

pheasant

pied wagtail

raven

redpoll

redwing

reed bunting

rook

siskin

sparrowhawk

stonechat

woodpigeon

wren

NOTE: Species may not have taken food.

*Data from IWC Annual Winter Garden Bird Feeding Survey.

NESTBOXES

If you have mature trees or high walls or a blank gable end to your house, putting up a nestbox to attract birds in summer is well worth considering. Like the bird table, you can buy one or make one. If you want to buy you have to be even more careful than with a bird table. Nestboxes, often referred to as bird houses, come in an incredible array of designs and colours and most on the market are over-priced and almost useless or even harmful to birds. There is the hybrid – half-nestbox, half-bird

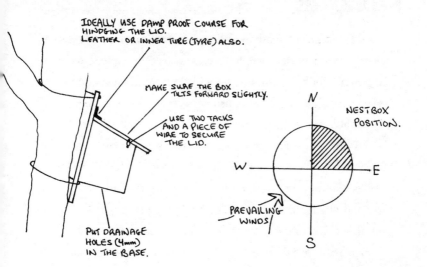

IDEALLY USE DAMP PROOF COURSE FOR HINDGING THE LID.
LEATHER OR INNER TUBE (TYRE) ALSO.

MAKE SURE THE BOX TILTS FORWARD SLIGHTLY.

USE TWO TACKS AND A PIECE OF WIRE TO SECURE THE LID.

PUT DRAINAGE HOLES (4mm) IN THE BASE.

NESTBOX POSITION.

N ... *W* ... *E* ... *S*

PREVAILING WINDS

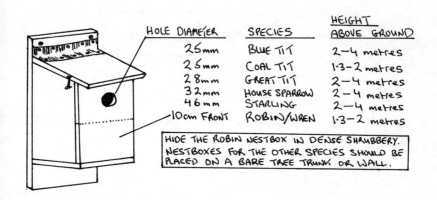

HOLE DIAMETER	SPECIES	HEIGHT ABOVE GROUND
25mm	BLUE TIT	2—4 metres
25mm	COAL TIT	1·3—2 metres
28mm	GREAT TIT	2—4 metres
32mm	HOUSE SPARROW	2—4 metres
46mm	STARLING	2—4 metres
10cm FRONT	ROBIN/WREN	1·3—2 metres

HIDE THE ROBIN NESTBOX IN DENSE SHRUBBERY.
NESTBOXES FOR THE OTHER SPECIES SHOULD BE PLACED ON A BARE TREE TRUNK OR WALL.

20 cm	25cm	20cm	24cm	16cm	45cm	
SIDE	SIDE	FRONT	ROOF	BASE	BACK	15 cm.

26cm 20cm

table – which is usually no good for either purpose. Then there are the nestboxes that are too small or so completely sealed that, if you are lucky enough to get a bird nesting in it, not only will you be unable to check the progress of your lodgers but you will be unable to clean it out in the winter without dismantling it. Birds rarely use the same nestbox twice if the old nest is not removed (usually in early October). Then if you do find what looks like a proper nestbox (see illustration) it will probably be so well-crafted that there will be no drainage holes at the bottom to allow any rain which gets into the box to drain away.

The main requirements for a good nestbox are that it has a lid that can be opened or removed and that it has roughly the dimensions and hole-size as one of those illustrated.

Ideally, nestboxes should be sited in a quiet place, 2.5 metres to 3.5 metres off the ground on a tree trunk or on the gable of a house. A new nestbox should be put up between October and the end of January. It should not be within reach of children, who once shown it will not leave it alone. It should not be placed in a bush, as most birds that use nestboxes like a clear area around the entrance. Do not nail the box to a living tree; instead, use plastic-coated wire or strong string, and remember to loosen the wire each year. If you do not have a suitable place, a neighbour or friend might. Always put the nestbox facing between the north and east away from hot summer sun, and from Ireland's prevailing winds and the worst of our wet weather. Don't be disappointed if your new box is not occupied in the first year. It may take two or even three years for a lodger to move in, and it is advisable to put up more than one box to increase your chances of success. In the winter your nestbox might be used as a roosting site for small birds such as wrens, so after some ongoing maintenance and repairs in early October put your nestbox back in place. Sixty-four wrens were counted entering a nest box on one winter's evening!

GARDENING

After providing the food, water, and somewhere to nest you can, if you have a garden, make your home into a haven for birds and other creatures by planting flowers and shrubs that attract birds. With so many wild areas being lost to 'development', gardens will increasingly become sanctuaries for birds, so why not make them more attractive.

Before discussing what plants to grow there are a few points to remember when considering wildlife gardening.

1. Take the minimalist approach. Use chemicals in the garden only when absolutely necessary. Insecticides and slug pellets can prove fatal to birds.
2. A wildlife garden does not mean surrendering your property to every 'weed', creepy-crawly and furry animal in the neighbourhood.
3. Remember, you cannot expect to have a clinically-kept garden and birds everywhere at the same time.

If you have a compost heap, a rough boundary and some berry-bearing bushes, you will be well-rewarded with a greater variety of birds in your garden all year round.

An area 30cm wide running the length of the hedge or boundary wall, which is mowed once or twice a year, will provide an excellent feeding habitat for birds. If you are tempted to sow wild meadowflower seeds, make sure they are of Irish origin to avoid introducing unwanted foreign species.

There are many shrubs and trees which will provide food for wild birds during the autumn and winter months. Trees to be recommended include willows, oaks, silver birch, poplar, hazel, field maple, alder and rowan. If you have not got one of these, put one in now. Most are fast-growing and will not grow very big. If possible, leave some leaf litter on the ground, under shrubs or in one corner of the garden. Birds such as blackbirds and song thrushes catch earthworms and insects under the dead leaves during the winter.

There are many shrubs that are beautiful to look at and also provide food for birds. The best-known is the buddleia which attracts butterflies and a host of other insects which birds eat. Shrubs and hedges provide shelter and roosting-places for birds, insects for food in the spring and summer, and berries through the winter. Other shrubs to be recommended are cotoneaster, hawthorn, holly, climbing rose, ivy, elder, honeysuckle, privet, crab apple and berberis.

A well-stocked herbaceous border will not only add colour to your garden but will also attract butterflies and insects and later seeds for birds to feed on. Flowers to be recommended are aubretia, balsam, cosmos, cornflower, candytuft, clarkia, evening primrose, forget-me-not, foxglove, honesty, lobelia, lavender, Michaelmas daisy, marjoram, primrose, sedum, snapdragon, sweet rocket, sunflower and thyme.

If you do not have a garden, window-boxes or plant-pots filled with flowers recommended above will not only brighten up your home but will also provide an oasis for birds. If you buy a Christmas tree every year and you have only a yard, put the dead tree in one corner. It will provide shelter and a roost site for birds coming to feed.

Even if you are only able to carry out some of the recommendations above, your garden will be a better place for birds.

WHERE TO NEXT?

Beyond your home, birdwatching becomes more challenging. The more habitats you visit the greater the variety of birds you will encounter. Do not rush around trying to see as many different species as quickly as possible. You will only end up confused and will probably mis-identify some of the birds you see. Start slowly, first with your neighbourhood, for example, the local park, pond or lake, wood or beach. Go there as often as you can and you will gradually get to know the birds of that habitat. Find out from the IWC or the RSPB where their nearest branch or group is. Non-members are usually welcome to attend meetings and outings, and you will find out where the best birdwatching sites in your area are.

WHEN TO BIRDWATCH

Remember that certain times of the day and year are better for birds than others. For watching seabirds away from breeding colonies, a trip to a headland in spring or autumn at early morning or evening when onshore winds are fairly strong can be rewarding. (Bring your rain gear!) Winter is by far the best season to look for waders and ducks because during our summer almost all have deserted our shores for their breeding grounds further north. Waders that feed on exposed mud and sand are best looked for just before or after high tide. They will be more concentrated on the small feeding areas still available and closest to a suitable viewing point. Dawn is by far the best time of day to observe land birds because most have been asleep all night and are hungry and therefore very active at first light. During the breeding season most birds sing best at dawn. Also most people are still in bed so human disturbance is at a minimum. Dusk can be good too but not as rewarding as dawn. Night-time is good for some species such as owls. Some other birds call at night, for example herons and crows. Birds on migration also call at night. Listen in March for the sound of curlews flying north. In late autumn and winter, the high, thin call of redwings on migration can be heard. During the winter almost any time of day will do because the day is so short. Looking for woodland birds during the summer can be very frustrating because thick leaf cover affords only brief views. Early spring and autumn are the best times.

THINGS TO DO

Put out a bird feeder. Put out water. Plant a buddleia. These three suggestions will dramatically increase the birdlife visiting your home. If you have a cat, put an elastic collar and bell on its neck. This will save the lives of many birds.

Do's and Don't's

- Always remember that the welfare of the birds comes first.
- Always bring your notebook and pen or pencil and record what birds you see, how many you see, and where you see them.
- Always be prepared for a sudden change in the weather.
- Always let someone know where you are going and roughly when you should be back. If you get really hooked on birdwatching, time-keeping can become difficult and fading light is usually the only thing that will definitely bring a day's birdwatching to an end, unless you decide to go looking for owls or listed night migrants, in which case you might never get home!
- Never look at the sun with binoculars or a telescope. It is EXTREMELY dangerous.
- Never point binoculars in the direction of other people.
- Never point binoculars, telescopes or cameras in the direction of houses.
- Never keep your binoculars, telescope or camera in its case when birdwatching.
- Never try to use binoculars with one hand. It is impossible to keep them steady and observe detail.
- Follow the country code – see below.

THE COUNTRY CODE

- GUARD AGAINST FIRE

- FASTEN ALL GATES

- KEEP TO PATHS ACROSS FARM LAND

- AVOID DAMAGING FENCES, HEDGES
  AND WALLS

- LEAVE NO LITTER

- KEEP NOISE TO A MINIMUM

- SAFEGUARD WATER SUPPLIES

- PROTECT WILDLIFE, PLANTS AND TREES

- GO CAREFULLY ON COUNTRY ROADS

- RESPECT THE LIFE OF THE COUNTRYSIDE

- ALWAYS SEEK PERMISSION TO ENTER LAND

FIRST AID FOR BIRDS

Almost everybody at some time or another comes across a bird that looks injured or abandoned. Most people are afraid to go near the bird and don't know what to do with it. Birds are delicate creatures and in most cases if injured or sick cannot be rehabilitated, even in the hands of the specialist.

YOUNG BIRDS

If you find a young bird, the best advice is to leave it alone. All young birds eventually get too big for the nest, and have to move out. They will stay on a branch or on the ground, not far from the nest, and wait for the parents to return to feed them. They may look as if they are in trouble but are almost always quite all right. Many species such as waterbirds, waders and seabirds have young that leave the nest the day they are born, relying on the camouflage of their down and feathers to hide them until their parents return with food. If the bird is in obvious danger from traffic, cats, etc. move it as short a distance as possible to safety. Resist the temptation to bring it home. The parents will find it when it calls for food. Even if the bird looks orphaned, it

How to feed a young bird.

is best to leave it where it is and return the following day. If it still looks in trouble, only then consider bringing it home.

Raising an orphaned bird is a very difficult task requiring a firm commitment of time and energy, and your best efforts might still end in failure. The young bird must be kept in a ventilated box in a warm quiet place. Make a 'nest' for unfeathered birds from strips of material or newspaper (replace regularly). A mixture of soaked, crushed biscuit, scrambled egg, thin strips of meat offal or a few pieces of cut-up earthworm will do for most young birds. Natural foods such as small insects can also be given. The moisture in the food provides enough water for the bird. Multivitamin drops used for human babies should be added to ensure healthy bone development. If you are fortunate enough to live near a pet shop, they might sell suitable food and vitamin supplements. A pair of blunt tweezers is ideal for feeding the young bird. Very gently tipping its bill will usually make it beg and if it will not cooperate get someone to open its mouth with thumb and forefinger. Put the food gently but firmly into its mouth. Young birds will eat up to their own weight in food every day and should be fed small quantities hourly during daylight only. Apart from owls, almost all birds feed their young only during daylight. Baby bird droppings are produced in neat, 'no-mess' sacs and should be removed immediately. Once the bird is old enough to jump about, put it in a cage and provide food with less moisture in a small dish and some water in a very shallow container or ideally in a budgie water dispenser. Dipping its beak in the water will usually lead to the bird drinking for itself.

Release the bird as soon as it appears ready and able to fly. Do this in good weather and as early in the morning as possible, in a safe place close to the spot where you found it. Leave it in its cage for a while before you let it go so it can become accustomed to its new surroundings. You might need to put out some food for a few days to help it adapt to the big wide world.

INJURED BIRDS

The following advice should be followed if you come across what seems to be an injured bird. If the bird is caught in something like fishing line or discarded net, try to cut the bird out rather than untangling it, which can do more harm than good. If possible wear a pair of gloves, especially when dealing with larger birds, as they might cut you with an infected beak or foot.

Remember, birds that appear very badly injured can still be very lively so don't put your face too close to it as it might strike out and injure you. Be especially careful with long-necked species such as herons, cormorants and gannets.

Trying to pick up a bird of prey such as a hawk or owl is very dangerous. The talons are lightning fast and razor-sharp. Thick gloves are essential. If a bird like a kestrel gets its talons into your skin, its reflex action causes it to tighten its grip the more you struggle to get free. It is an extremely frightening and painful experience. Waving a rag near its talons will usually make it grab it, allowing you time to catch its legs as close to the body as possible. Try to put a sock or glove over its head as darkness will help calm the frightened bird.

The way to hold large and small birds is illustrated below. Transport the bird in a ventilated box or bag. If it is not possible to take it directly to a vet, take it home and put it in a warm, dark, and quiet place for a few hours before examining it.

Many birds that look injured are in fact only in shock or are stunned. At first they may not be able to stand or sit and may look almost dead, but after a few hours they can make an almost miraculous recovery.

Do not be tempted to check on the bird at regular intervals.

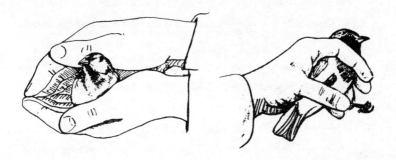

Different ways of holding small birds.

This will often finish off an already distressed bird. If the bird has improved but still looks unable to fly, leave it overnight and examine it first thing the next morning. If the bird has any superficial cuts, these should be treated with a mild antiseptic wipe. Anything more serious should really be seen by a vet. Broken wings are usually easy to fix, but only by a specialist and without proper antibiotic treatment most casualties will die within a matter of days.

If the bird looks like it only needs short-term care, it will have to be fed. As with the young bird it is advisable to give vitamin supplements. Try to identify the bird or at least try to establish what type of bird it is as this will determine what you should feed it. For example, finches, sparrows, buntings and doves should be fed bird seed. Ducks, geese and pheasants can be fed racing pigeon food or mixed corn. Crows and gulls will eat tinned dog food. Herons and most seabirds such as auks will eat fish sliced in strips. Birds of prey need strips of raw meat or dead day-old chicks. Provision of water is also important. Releasing rehabilitated birds is the same as that for young birds.

For a detailed treatment of this very complex subject Les Stoker's *St. Tiggywinkles Wildcare Handbook* (Chatto & Windus, 1992) is highly recommended.

The IWC and RSPB are not animal welfare organisations and do not have facilities for the care and rehabilitation of young, sick or injured birds, but they may be able to suggest a member in your area with experience and advice. A call to your local centre of the ISPCA or RSPCA may be worthwhile.

Identifying Ireland's
Common Birds

Species are arranged here in family order. Species have been chosen if they are common in the winter and/or breeding season. A few species have also been included if they are well known (e.g. corncrake) or are conspicuous or easy to identify (e.g. kingfisher) though not common.

KEY

- **SPECIES NAME**: This is given in English and in Irish – and any local names are also given (in brackets). The Latin name appears in Italics under the details.

Details: under the name you will find the following information:

- Best time to see the species:

  A = all year round **W** = winter **S** = summer.

- **L** = Length in centimetres of the bird from the tip of the bill to the middle of the end of the tail.

- **WS** = Length in centimetres of the wing span from wing tip to wing tip (where information is available).

- * = In the top twenty most widespread Irish breeding species list.

- **MAIN FEATURES** This section describes the main identification features of each species. For quick reference, sub-headings such as **Adult**, **Immature**, **Male**, **Female**, **Summer**, **Winter**, are used where there are distinct plumage differences. **In flight**: is used to highlight flight characteristics and plumage features not visible when the bird is at rest.

- **VOICE GUIDE** The song and call of each species is given. Phonetic translation is included only to give the reader a general idea of what type of sound the bird makes. Bear in mind that accent, and therefore the sound description, will be different for people from Antrim and from Kerry. It is hoped that the phonetic translation will point the reader in the right direction rather than purport to provide a definitive translation.

- **GENERAL INFORMATION** This section is intended to provide the reader with some additional information on the species which they have identified. The figures quoted on breeding and wintering populations are extracted from the *New Atlas of Breeding Birds in Britain and Ireland: 1988-91* (1993) and the *Winter Atlas of Birds of Britain and Ireland*, 1981-84 (1986). These two books are the result of detailed surveys coverning several years, by thousands of amateur and professional ornithologists in Britain and Ireland. Any figures quoted are conservative totals for each species.

- **CONFUSION SPECIES** This section indicates, where appropriate, other species which may be confused with the species being described. Only key differences are described.

Little Grebe (Dabchick) *Spágaire Tonn*

A   L = 25-29   WS = 40-45
Tachybaptus ruficollis (PLATE 2)

MAIN FEATURES Small diving bird. From a distance looks dark in colour. **Summer**: chestnut neck and ear coverts; creamy spot at base of the short bill. **Winter**: pale throat and light brown neck and breast. It has a characteristic shape with a fluffy rear end and buoyant appearance. **In flight**: all dark above. When disturbed will usually run along the surface of the water, with wings fluttering, to cover. Flight is fast and straight.

VOICE GUIDE Its call is a high, loud and long whinnying trill.

GENERAL INFORMATION Also known as the dabchick, this inconspicuous little waterbird is often overlooked. It can be found breeding in freshwater ponds and lakes. It does not like fast-running water. In the winter many move to coastal inshore waters. Dives for small fish and also to escape danger. It travels underwater using its strong, lobed feet set far back on the body.

Great Crested Grebe *Lúnadán*

W   L=46-51   WS=89-90
Podiceps cristatus (PLATE 4)

MAIN FEATURES Summer: unmistakeable in breeding plumage with long thin neck and striking head pattern with chestnut and black ear-tufts. **Winter**: dark crown; white face, neck and underside; dark grey-brown flanks; straight, pink dagger-shaped bill; thin dark line between the eye and the base of the bill. **In flight**: looks long-bodied; large white patches on the inner half of the wings; very fast wing beats and outstretched slightly drooping neck. When taking to the air it runs rapidly along the surface of the water for a couple of metres.

VOICE GUIDE Usually silent. Display call a guttural *krraaa-krraaa* ..., also a higher *aaah-aaah* ...

GENERAL INFORMATION A common winter visitor from the Continent. Found on the coast and in estuaries, usually in small flocks but sometimes over a hundred can be seen together. Like its cousin the little grebe, it is a diving bird though much larger than that species. It breeds on open fresh-water bodies mainly north of a line between Limerick and Dublin.

Fulmar *Fulmaire*

S   L=45-50   WS=102-112
Fulmarus glacialis (PLATE 1)

MAIN FEATURES White head, thick-necked; blue-grey or brown-grey above, white below; cigar-shaped body; light grey tail; stout bill. **In flight**: pale patches at base of primaries. Shallow stiff wing beats punctuated with glides. The stronger the wind the longer and more undulating the glides, and like its relative, the albatross, it glides effortlessly even in gale-force winds.

VOICE GUIDE Usually vocal only at the nest, when it makes a laughing, squawking chatter.

GENERAL INFORMATION Slightly smaller than a herring gull, this wanderer of the oceans is mainly a summer visitor to our shores. In the last century, this bird was very rare in Ireland but since 1900 it has spread to almost every sea-cliff of any height around our coast, nesting on ledges near the tops of the cliffs. It spends most of its time on the open seas looking for food on the surface of the water or offal from fishing boats.

CONFUSION SPECIES *Gulls* (PLATE 6): not stiff-winged in flight; bill narrower, body not cigar-shaped.

Gannet *Gainéad*

S   L=87-100   WS=165-180
Sula bassana (PLATE 1)

MAIN FEATURES Our largest seabird. **Adult**: unmistakeable with its brilliant white plumage, long narrow wings, black wing tips, pointed tail. Head is yellow, though not always very noticeable at a distance. Immature: dark brown, but identical in shape, gradually becoming whiter as they reach adulthood. This usually takes between four and six years. In flight: when not feeding, gannets fly in V formation or in single file just above the waves. Glides and soars in strong wind.

VOICE GUIDE At the breeding colony, a rapidly repeated *dirraaw-dirraaw-dirraaw ...*, varying slightly in pitch, forming a continuous chorus. Also heard when feeding in a flock over a shoal of fish.

GENERAL INFORMATION Usually seen around our coasts in summer, it spends the winter off the west coast of Africa, although a few do overwinter here. It nests in dense colonies on rocky off-shore islands, the most famous being on the IWC reserve of Little Skellig in County Kerry, where over 20,000 pairs breed each year. Away from the breeding colony it can be seen singly or in flocks. When it is feeding it dives from up to 30 metres, plunging with a splash to a depth of three or four metres. If fish are close to the surface it enters the water at a small angle. When it resurfaces it usually sits for a few seconds before running into the wind along the surface with outstretched wings when taking to the air.

Cormorant

(Billydiver) *Broigheall*

A   L=80-100   WS=130-160
Phalacrocorax carbo (PLATE 1)

MAIN FEATURES Adult: all black. In breeding plumage white 'diamond' on the thigh; orange and white throat patch. Thick snake-like neck; strong pale hook-tipped bill. **Immature**: pale belly and throat. Swims low in the water with slightly raised bill. **In flight**: runs along the surface of the water to take off. Flight is straight on, shallow, rapid wing beats with intermittent glides. Neck is slightly bent. Usually flies low over water but can fly very high on its own or in a group travelling in lines or Vs. Skis along the water when landing. It feeds on fish and when diving underwater disappears without much of a splash.

VOICE GUIDE Usually silent.

GENERAL INFORMATION The cormorant is a common bird of coast, estuaries, rivers and large lakes. As its nick-name suggests it is a diving bird, using its large strong, black, webbed feet to propel itself under the water. It breeds in colonies on sea cliffs and in trees on lake islands. Cormorants roost in trees, on small rocky islands or at the end of jetties or piers and can often be seen standing with their wings outstretched. It is often assumed that they are drying their water-logged wings but some believe that the wings are held out to aid the digestion of recently-swallowed prey, as they are sometimes seen with outstretched wings in the pouring rain.

CONFUSION SPECIES *Shag* (PLATE 1): see below.

Shag *Seaga*

A   L=65-80   WS=90-105

Phalacrocorax aristotelis (PLATE 1)

MAIN FEATURES Smaller, less robust version of the cormorant. In breeding plumage, distinctive forward-curling crown tufts, all dark plumage and thin yellow patch below the eye. In winter it loses its tufts and the yellow patch gets dull. Unlike the cormorant, immature birds are pale brown rather than grey-white below.

VOICE GUIDE Usually silent.

GENERAL INFORMATION It is far more coastal in its distribution, rarely going inland beyond river estuaries. Usually a solitary hunter and when diving its whole body lifts off the surface before going underwater. Can be found nesting on its own or in colonies and often prefers more inaccessible cliff ledges.

CONFUSION SPECIES *Cormorant* (PLATE 1): see above.

Grey Heron (Crane) *Corr Éisc*

A   L=90-98   WS=150-175

Ardea cinerea (PLATE 2)

MAIN FEATURES Large dagger-shaped bill; white head, with a thick black stripe from the eye to the back of the head; long neck; grey body; long legs. **Breeding plumage**: adults grow long thin feathers on neck and breast and two long black feathers on the back of the head. Bill changes colour from dull yellow-orange to a bright pink. **Immature**: greyer plumage, duller bill. **In flight**: bowed wings, slow wing beats; neck tucked up and legs trailing beyond short tail. Wings and back grey with darker primaries and secondaries.

VOICE GUIDE When it takes off or is disturbed it gives a loud *fraank* call. Some of the sounds of adults and young at the nest, heard at any time of day or night, are like a fairy-tale monster or someone getting sick!

GENERAL INFORMATION Grey herons feed mainly on fish, frogs, small animals and occasionally insects. Often referred to as a 'crane' or 'Johnny-the-Bog', the grey heron is Ireland's tallest bird. It usually nests in colonies called heronries, which it frequents from January until late summer. It can often be seen silently stalking its prey on lake edges, in rivers and streams or on the coast. Sometimes it fishes in the middle of towns and cities. It is sometimes chased by crows and gulls.

Mute Swan *Eala Bhalbh (Geis)*

A   L=145-160   WS=208-235
Cygnus olor (PLATE 3)

Adult: All white. Male (cob) slightly larger than the female (pen), with larger black knob at the base of the orange-red bill. **Immature:** cygnets grey-brown; dull grey-pink bill; acquiring adult plumage in the second year. **In flight**: take-off is laboured, running along the surface of the water for a few metres with powerful wingbeats. The long neck is held straight out and the wings make a buzzing sound. Skiis along the water when landing.

VOICE GUIDE Not as silent as its name suggests. Greeting call is a soft wheezing *whe-aarrrr*, also lower coughing sounds. Hisses when defending territory or young.

GENERAL INFORMATION Our largest bird, the mute swan needs no introduction. Found all year round on lakes, slow-flowing rivers, canals, and estuaries, it is often quoted as a species that pairs for life. This is untrue and the story that if one of the pair dies the other will die of a broken heart is also untrue. It usually moves only short distances though some have been shown to travel over 250 kilometres. It is very defensive of its breeding territory and will chase off any other mute swans that intrude. A large nest is built and between five and eleven young are hatched in late May or early June. Up to 33 percent of cygnets will die in the first two months of life. Mute swans will remain as a family unit until the young are chased away by the parents in the following spring when the young birds are replacing the grey-brown feathers with white ones. Mute swans usually take three or four years to mature and can live for up to twenty years.

CONFUSION SPECIES *Whooper* and *Bewick's Swans* (PLATE 3): scarce winter visitors; yellow and black bills; hold their necks straight. Mute swan when swimming has a curved neck and holds the head tilted downwards.

Brent Goose *Gé Dhubh*

W   L=58-62   WS=115-125
Branta bernicula (PLATE 4)

MAIN FEATURES Adult: Black head, neck and breast; white 'gill' marks on the side of the neck; upper parts dark grey-brown; tail white with a narrow black edge; belly light grey-brown, undertail white; legs and short bill black. **Immature**: similar to adults but usually lacks the white neck marks and has white edges to some of the wing feathers. **In flight**: looks dark except for the white on the tail and undertail which is very noticeable. Fast wing beats and usually does not fly in classic V formation, the flock shape ranging from long loose lines to bunched groups, often flying low over water.

VOICE GUIDE In flocks a muted, quivering *grough*, often silent on their own.

GENERAL INFORMATION The brent goose is the smallest of our wintering geese. The species is divided up into distinct races and those visiting Ireland are almost all of the pale-bellied race. It breeds in Arctic Canada, many on Queen Elizabeth Island and Bathurst Island in northern Canada. Birds arrive here as early as late August with most here by the end of October. Unlike other geese it is found regularly on estuaries. It favours eel grass and can often be seen up-ending like a mallard to reach its food when covered by the tide. In recent years it has been seen feeding in increasing numbers on pasture and stubble fields, golf courses, playing fields and park grasslands. The total mid-winter population in Ireland is about 20,000 but is highly variable from year to year, depending on breeding success. The largest winter concentrations are at Strangford Lough, Dublin Bay and Lough Foyle. Small flocks occur in many estuaries, harbours and bays around the coast but are very scarce in counties Cork, south Kerry, north Wexford-south Wicklow and Antrim. The brent goose has been well studied in Ireland and it has been shown that like other geese it remains in family groups throughout the winter. It has also been discovered that food availability mainly determines its movements around the island. It is possible to find it singly or in small numbers away from its regular locations in suitable habitats anywhere in Ireland.

CONFUSION SPECIES *Barnacle Goose* (PLATE 4): creamy white face; paler, grey wings; confined mainly to the coast of Mayo and Donegal. *Canada Goose* (NOT ILLUSTRATED): white chin strap; brown wings and back; large size; found on some ponds and lakes in towns, cities and on estates. *Greenland White-fronted Goose* (PLATE 4): grey-brown with white undertail; irregular black bands on the belly; white forehead (adults only), orange bill and legs; largest concentrations in Wexford, smaller flocks in the midlands, west and north.

Shelduck *Lacha Bhreach*

W   L=58-71   WS=110-133
Tadorna tadorna (PLATE 4)

MAIN FEATURES Adult: large size; mainly white body; black head; red bill and pink legs rule out confusion with any other duck. Females are smaller than males, lack the red knob on the base of the bill and have almost no black on the belly. **Immature**: newly-fledged young are similar in shape to the adults but are black and white, lacking the bright colours of the adults. **In flight**: broad pale chestnut breast band; black 'braces' on the back; black primaries and secondaries. Found mostly in estuaries, with a preference for mudflats.

VOICE GUIDE Usually vocal only during the breeding season. Loud calls include a rapid, guttural, laughing *agh,agh,agh,agh* ... lasting several seconds. Also a high liquid *tiew-tiew* ... with a high whistle.

GENERAL INFORMATION Shelduck nest in holes and cavities of all types, from rabbit burrows to discarded plastic drums. Clutches can contain up to 11 young and are often protected in a crêche containing two to four broods guarded by one or two adults. After breeding almost all our shelduck migrate to the Wadden Sea off the North German coast to moult, returning to Irish estuaries from September onwards. Searches for small snails and worms in mud, moving its bill from side to side in a scythe-like fashion.

Wigeon *Lacha Rua*

W   L=45-51   WS=75-86
Anas penelope (PLATE 3)

GENERAL INFORMATION Male: round, dark red-brown head; conspicuous creamy forehead and crown. Mainly grey body; grey-pink breast; white patch at rear of the flanks; undertail coverts black. Short blue-grey bill with black tip. **Female**: drab grey-brown; pale belly; identical to the male in shape. **In flight**: rises quickly from water or land. White wing patches on the inner part of the wing (males only), pale belly.

VOICE GUIDE The males utter a distinctive whistling *feeoow* while the female makes a lower guttural sound.

GENERAL INFORMATION The wigeon is a medium-sized surface-feeding duck seen mainly in winter. It can be found inland or on the coast, usually in estuaries, where it feeds on grasses and algae. Rarely encountered on its own, this duck can be seen in flocks of over 1,000 birds. Most of our wigeon come here from Iceland and Continental Europe to spend the winter, departing in early March and returning in autumn. There is a small breeding population primarily along the river Shannon. One way to remember how to identify male wigeon is to think of pigeon, because the woodpigeon has similar colours.

Teal *Praslacha*

W   L=34-38   WS=58-64
Anas crecca (PLATE 3)

MAIN FEATURES Male: chestnut head and neck; dark green eye patches extending down the side of the neck; pale yellow undertail outlined in black, horizontal white line above the closed wing. **Female**: all brown. **In flight**: rises quickly, rapid wing beats, plain appearance, green speculum on males and females. (The speculum, which is a specially-coloured area on the wings of some birds, is usually visible only at close range or in good light conditions.)

VOICE GUIDE In winter flocks these birds can be very noisy. The male makes a short low bell-sounding *krreet*, the female makes a much higher quack.

GENERAL INFORMATION This small surface-feeding duck is widespread and common both inland and on the coast in winter. Once a common breeding bird, it has declined significantly in recent years. In the winter Irish birds are joined by teal from Iceland, Continental Europe and from as far away as northwest Siberia and occasionally North America.

Mallard *Lacha Fhiáin*

A L=51-62 WS=81-98
Anas platyrhynchos (PLATE 3)

MAIN FEATURES Male: iridescent blue-green head; thin white neck ring; yellow bill and unusual up-curled feathers at base of whitish tail. **Female**: dull brown; identical in shape to the male; bill reddish-orange with variable amounts of dark brown; lacks curled tail feathers. **In flight**: white-bordered blue speculum on both male and female. During moult – mainly in mid-July – males resemble females except for the yellow-green bill.

VOICE GUIDE The female makes a wide variety of calls ranging from the classic *quack* to a call that sounds as if it was laughing at you. The male makes a much quieter *wheep* sound.

GENERAL INFORMATION Our most common surface feeding duck, about the size of a chicken, the mallard can be found almost anywhere in Ireland where there is water, from estuaries to rivers and lakes and even in parks in the middle of towns and cities. Young birds can dive, especially when frightened. Often interbreeds with domestic ducks, especially in towns and cities, resulting in the most bizarre offspring and an identification nightmare for the beginner.

Irish mallard rarely travel very far but are joined by mallard from Iceland and Scandinavia in the winter.

Tufted Duck *Lacha Dhubh*

W L=40-47 WS=67-73
Aythya fuligula (PLATE 4)

MAIN FEATURES Small diving duck. **Male**: long tuft of black feathers sticking out of the back of the head; all black with a white belly and flanks;

purple-blue sheen on the black feathers visible at close range; light blue-grey bill, black tip (also referred to as a nail); bright golden-yellow eye. **Female**: dark brown; pale belly and varying degrees of paleness around the base of the bill. **In flight**: fast and straight, broad white wing bar, white belly and underwing.

VOICE GUIDE Usually silent. In courtship the male makes quiet whistling sound. The female growls.

GENERAL INFORMATION These birds are sometimes found in town and city parks and often feed in the company of another diving duck, the pochard. They nest mainly in the northern half of the country. In winter over 5,000 birds can be seen on Lough Neagh. Local birds are joined by birds from other north European countries. Recent surveys indicated that tufted ducks are declining in Ireland.

Red-breasted Merganser *Tumaire*

W L=51-62 WS=70-86
Mergus serrator (PLATE 4)

MAIN FEATURES Diving duck. **Male**: long spiky feathers sticking out of the back of its dark green head; broad white neck collar; streaked pink-grey breast. Variable amounts of white visible on the closed wing. Long thin red bill; red legs; red eye. **Female**: brown head; short spikes; pale throat, breast and belly; grey-brown body. **In flight**: fast and straight with rapid wing beats, large white wing patches and stretched neck appearance.

VOICE GUIDE No sound usually.

GENERAL INFORMATION Mainly seen during the winter months around our coastline. This handsome diving duck, with a shape more like a shag, feeds mainly on fish which it catches underwater with its long thin bill. Rarely found alone, sometimes up to 200 can be seen together in sheltered areas along the coast and in estuaries. Irish birds are joined by mergansers from Iceland and Scandinavia. This species breeds mainly in the western half of Ireland and has declined in numbers in recent years.

Sparrowhawk *Spioróg*

A   L=28-38   WS=60-75
Accipter nisus (PLATE 8)

MAIN FEATURES Size of a rook. **Male**: blue-grey above; barred white and orange below; underside of tail, broadly barred light and dark grey-brown. **Female**: larger than the male; dark grey-brown above; pale supercilium (eyebrow); barred white and brown below. **In flight**: broad blunt-ended wings; long slightly round-ended tail; rapid wing beats with short glides; soars but does not hover.

VOICE GUIDE Varied repertoire during the breeding season including a loud high *wa-kaa-kaa-kaa* ..., each phrase lasting about two seconds, followed by a brief pause and repeat. When the young are begging for food they make a high squeaking *weee-weee-weee* ... Silent outside the breeding season.

GENERAL INFORMATION This and the next species (kestrel) are the most abundant birds of prey in Ireland. The name gives a clue to its food or prey, mainly small birds. It is a resident bird in Ireland and can be seen in winter and summer, circling like a vulture looking for its next meal. The bird prefers to hunt in wooded areas where it ambushes its prey. It also hunts along hedgerows and almost all birds of prey attacking birds in gardens have been identified as sparrowhawks. There is some evidence in recent years that it is declining as a breeding species in Ireland though the cause is unknown.

Kestrel *Pocaire Gaoithe*

A   L=33-39   WS=65-80
Falco tinnunculus (PLATE 8)

MAIN FEATURES Male: grey head; grey tail with a black band on the end; dark primaries; rusty red wing coverts and back; body buff with dark streaking; underwing pale. **Female** and **immature**: duller brown instead of rusty red above; more heavily streaked. **In flight**: hovers when searching for food. The kestrel has narrower and more pointed wings than the sparrowhawk.

VOICE GUIDE Vocal during the breeding season, near its nest. A loud sharp rapid *kee-kee-kee-keee* ...

GENERAL INFORMATION The kestrel is a perfect example of how a bird can be identified by its 'jizz' alone (see page 203), at any distance. Its ability to hover in most wind conditions, with tail spread and wings held high, makes it unique among Irish birds of prey. Unlike the sparrowhawk it feeds mainly on rodents, occasionally taking small birds and insects. It is resident and unlike the sparrowhawk nests in a wide variety of habitats, e.g. trees, ruins, cliff ledges and even on large buildings. It breeds throughout the country and can often be seen hunting next to roads, especially where there are large grass verges. There is some evidence of a small decline in recent years but this requires further investigation.

Peregrine *Seabhac Seilge*

A   L=39-50   WS=95-115
Falco peregrinus (PLATE 8)

MAIN FEATURES Larger than a rook. **Adult**: dark blue-grey upper parts; slightly paler rump; underparts barred black and white; head, dark with noticeable broad dark moustachial stripes and white throat. **Immature**: darker and browner above, heavily streaked below. **In flight**: short-tailed with broad-based and very pointed wings; stoops (dives) on prey with wings almost fully closed at high speed.

VOICE GUIDE Its song includes a high, irritating, squeaking *kaw-kik-kaw-tieu* ... Alarm call is a high drawn-out *kwaugh* cry repeated with variable pitch.

GENERAL INFORMATION The word 'peregrine' comes from the Latin 'to wander' and is very apt for this bird, our most powerful and speedy raptor. The recent history of the species in Ireland and abroad illustrates well the need for us to be very careful when introducing chemicals into the natural food chain. The use of organochlorine insecticides such as DDT in the late fifties and sixties threatened the future of this species in Europe, so dramatic was its decline. Thankfully these chemicals are now under tight legal control and the peregrine is making a comeback. It nests on sea cliffs and inland quarries and occasionally on large buildings in cities. Irish peregrines are mainly resident. Feeds mainly on small-to-medium-sized birds which it catches by stooping from a height with wings almost closed at speeds up to 300km per hour, hitting its prey with such force as to kill it instantly.

Pheasant *Coilleach Coille*

A   L=53-89   WS=70-90
Phasianus colchicus (PLATE 11)

MAIN FEATURES Male: unmistakeable red face, white neck ring; large body; short legs; tail longer than its body. **Female**: mottled brown, shorter tail. A fast runner and usually flies only when absolutely necessary. **In flight**: rapid wing beats make a whirring sound, rarely travels more than a hundred metres before diving for cover.

VOICE GUIDE The best time of year to hear a pheasant is in late spring or early summer when the cock crows, making a sound like a loud rusty gate.

GENERAL INFORMATION Believed to have been introduced into Ireland around 1590 probably from Britain or Western Europe, but originating in the Caucasus where pheasants lack a neck ring, and later China where they have a white neck ring. A very distinctive, big bird, often seen flying over roads or exploding from cover at the edge of a field. Found in good numbers everywhere in Ireland except west Mayo and parts of the north.

The 'wild' population is supplemented by the release of hand-reared birds by gun clubs and up to 200,000 are shot each year.

CONFUSION SPECIES *Corncrake* (PLATE 11): extremely rare; half its size; rusty-brown wings; rasping *crex-crex* call.

Water Rail *Traonach Uisce*

A   L=22-28   WS=38-45
Rallus aquaticus (PLATE 2)

MAIN FEATURES Slightly smaller than a blackbird. *Upper parts*: streaked black; brown back and wings. *Underside*: dark grey face, neck and breast; belly and flanks heavily barred black and white; undertail coverts white; eyes and long slightly down-curved bill are red; legs and large feet dull pink. **In flight**: legs hang down; usually only flies a short distance if disturbed.

VOICE GUIDE The easiest way to identify this secretive bird is to listen for its loud grunting and squealing pig-like call coming from a reed bed or other waterside vegetation. The best time to hear it is at dawn or dusk. Also calls at night.

GENERAL INFORMATION Will be seen only if it has to cross a ditch or open ground between reed beds, or when the weather becomes freezing cold. Its small size and wedge-shaped body make it well-suited for life in dense vegetation. Feeds on insects, seed and other vegetable matter. In severe, cold weather it can be found away from reed beds.

CONFUSION SPECIES *Corncrake* (PLATE 11): extremely rare; stubby pink bill; no white; rusty-brown wings.

Corncrake *Traonach*

L=27-30   WS=45-53
Crex crex (PLATE 11)

MAIN FEATURES Difficult to see; the males utter a loud unmusical rasping *crex-crex* call best heard in the middle of the night. Usually seen in flight only when disturbed, its rusty red rounded wings, very short tail and long trailing legs identify this bird of damp meadows.

VOICE GUIDE See above.

GENERAL INFORMATION Now almost extinct in Ireland. It is hard to believe that once this bird was as synonymous with the start of summer as the swallow. In 1994 there were less than 180 pairs left in Ireland; in the 1950s it could be heard in almost every meadow during summer.

Changes in farming practices are considered to be the main cause of its decline in Ireland, the move from hay-making to silage and the advent of tractor-drawn cutting machines giving this very reluctant flier little chance to escape.

The Shannon callows (low-lying meadows), where the IWC have a reserve, is one of the last strongholds of this summer visitor, which has all but disappeared from the rest of the island.

CONFUSION SPECIES *Pheasant* (PLATE 11): twice its size; light brown wings; long tail.

Moorhen *Cearc Uisce*

A   L=32-35   WS=50-55
Gallinula chloropus (PLATE 2)

MAIN FEATURES Adult: bright red forehead shield; red and yellow bill and dark plumage, apart from some white streaks on the flanks and on the undertail; large feet. **Immature**: browner and paler, lacking the brightly-coloured forehead and bill. Downy young are all black with a red and yellow bill. **In flight**: rarely flies and when frightened or in danger runs along the surface of the water with neck outstretched and wings flapping furiously. It will make for the nearest cover of reeds or other waterside vegetation.

VOICE GUIDE Makes many sounds. Usually a loud harsh *krrrek* or a fast double noted *ka-kik*.

GENERAL INFORMATION About the size of a jackdaw, the moorhen is one of our most common breeding waterbirds, with 75,000 pairs on freshwater areas of all sizes. They have been known to lay up to 21 eggs, but seven or eight is the average clutch size. It is easy to identify as it feeds in the open on and around ponds, rivers and lakes on a wide range of plant and insect matter. In the winter, Irish moorhens are joined by birds from Continental Europe. Future threats include land drainage and predation by mink.

CONFUSION SPECIES *Coot* (PLATE 2): **see below.**

Coot *Cearc Cheannann*

A   L=36-38   WS=70-80
Fulica atra (PLATE 2)

MAIN FEATURES Adult: black plumage; conspicuous white bill and forehead shield; dark red eyes; large, lobed green-grey feet.

Immature: paler than adults, especially on the head, neck and breast. Downy chicks are dark brown with an orange-red head. **In flight**: similar to moorhen. Dives regularly, mainly for vegetable matter, though some invertebrates are also eaten.

VOICE GUIDE Sounds include a loud short *krouw*, repeated mechanically, with several intermittent brief high-pitched nasal whistles.

GENERAL INFORMATION Not as widespread or common as the moorhen, prefers larger bodies of freshwater. Fights with other coots in defence of its breeding territory. Coots always bring their food to the surface before eating and other waterbirds and gulls will often wait nearby to snatch a free meal. In winter, unlike the moorhen, can often be seen in flocks on larger bodies of freshwater. Coots from the Continent come here in severe winters. When the weather is very cold they can even be seen on estuaries. The expression 'bald as a coot', comes from the fact that the forehead shield is not made up of small white feathers but of bare skin.

CONFUSION SPECIES *Moorhen* (PLATE 2): red and yellow bill; broken white flank line and white on the undertail; does not dive.

Oystercatcher *Roilleach*

W   L=40-50   WS=80-86
Haematopus ostralegus (PLATE 5)

MAIN FEATURES Large wader. **Adult**: black-and-white plumage; stout pink legs; long straight orange-red bill; indistinct white half-collar in winter. **Immature**: orange bill with a dark tip, gradually becoming the colour of an adult as they mature; broad white half-collar until they are two or three years old. **In flight**: black-and-white striped wings; white triangle on the back; white tail with a black band on the end.

VOICE GUIDE Makes a very loud, single-noted piping call, repeated often and sometimes speeding up at the end. Noisy piping sessions are often heard when several birds form a loose circle, with necks stretched outward and upward and bills pointing towards the ground.

GENERAL INFORMATION Breeds along our coastline though almost absent from the south coast west of Dungarvan. Small numbers also nest inland. In winter Irish birds are joined by oystercatchers from Scotland, Iceland, and the Faeroes. Flocks of over a hundred are not uncommon. It is very territorial when nesting and during the winter. When feeding will often chase off other birds while searching for shellfish and worms on mudflats, sandy shores, rocky shores and grassy fields, with a particular fondness for sports fields. One word to describe a group of oystercatchers in flight is a squadron, their habit of flying rapidly in straight lines or in V formation, often very low, has a military discipline about it.

Ringed Plover *Feadóg an Fháinne*

W   L=18-20   WS=48-57
Charadrius hiaticula (PLATE 5)

MAIN FEATURES A small wader. **Adult**: distinctive head and breast pattern; forehead white, surrounded by a black face mask; white eyebrow; continuous white neck collar; black breast band; body dark sandy brown above, white below; bill short and stubby, orange with a black tip; legs pale orange-red. **Immature** and **adults in winter**: all-dark bill; olive-grey legs; incomplete breast band. **In flight**: white wing bar, white edge to dark tail.

VOICE GUIDE Its call is a loud clear, soft *twoo-ip*. Also repeated with descending pitch. Song includes a rapid, muted *ti-wou*, repeated many times for several seconds and lowering in pitch towards the end.

GENERAL INFORMATION This small plover breeds mainly around our coast, with small numbers on western lakes. As a breeding bird it is more common north of a line from Dublin to Limerick. It prefers to nest just above the high water line on shingle or sandy beaches. Increased human disturbance due to many people walking beaches during the breeding season has led to a decline in recent years. The presence of a breeding pair is easy to prove as the adults are very noisy and pretend to have a broken wing to lure you away from the excellently-camouflaged eggs. The young are able to leave the nest almost immediately and are equally difficult to locate. From early autumn, flocks of up to 250 birds can be counted on sandy beaches and in some estuaries. Ringed plovers from Britain, the Baltic, Iceland, Greenland and northern Russia join our own at various times throughout autumn and winter. It feeds by sight, mainly on worms and crustaceans.

Lapwing *Pilibín*

W   L=28-31   WS=70-76
Vanellus vanellus (PLATE 5)

MAIN FEATURES Adult: only Irish wader with along thin crest, shorter on females. Complex black-and-white face pattern, black breast, white belly, chestnut undertail coverts. Wings broad, round and black, apart from small white patches on the outer four primaries. Iridescent blue and green on wings and back; tail white with a black end; bill short, straight, stubby and black; legs are long and pink. **In flight**: at a distance a flock of lapwing 'twinkles' as the white bellies are revealed and obscured by the dark wings.

VOICE GUIDE Its call is usually an eerie squeaky sound or, as another of its names suggests, a squeaky *peewit*.

GENERAL INFORMATION The acrobatic display flights and calls during the breeding season are spectacular. In Ireland it breeds mainly in the midlands and north. A serious decline in breeding birds in the last 20 years is largely due to changes in agricultural practices, where intermixed grasslands have been replaced by autumn-grown cereal crops and stocking rates on grassland have increased.

In winter the lapwing is our most widespread wader, with flocks turning up anywhere, though usually not far from wetland areas. Irish birds are joined mainly by birds from northern Britain and in very cold weather also by lapwing from Continental Europe. Flocks of up to 10,000 can sometimes be seen and up to 250,000 winter in Ireland each year. It feeds on invertebrates and has a preference for ploughed fields, though in cold weather it can turn up almost anywhere.

Dunlin *Breacóg*

W   L=16-22   WS=35-40
Calidris alpina (PLATE 5)

MAIN FEATURES Small wader. **Summer**: complex pattern of browns, black and greys above, characteristic black belly patch, streaked face and breast below. **Winter**: grey-brown above and white below; dark

streaking on the breast; bill long, slightly curved and black; legs black. **In flight**: thin white wing bar; dark tail and dark line running through white rump. Rarely seen alone, it feeds day and night where mud and sand are exposed, mainly on small invertebrates living close to the surface.

VOICE GUIDE Call is a rather weak, grating *treee*.

GENERAL INFORMATION In winter no other shore bird is found here in greater numbers. It is mainly coastal though also found inland in small numbers. Anywhere there is mud you are almost certain to see these small wanderers from almost every country in northern Europe. In mid-winter, up to half the total west European population of dunlin are found in Ireland and Britain. Flocks can range in size from less than 100 to over 10,000. Many birds also use Ireland as a stepping-stone in spring and autumn on their journeys between their wintering grounds in north-west Africa and their breeding grounds in northern Europe. Breeds in small numbers in estuarine marshes and bogs in the north-western half of the island.

CONFUSION SPECIES Some other species of small wader can superficially resemble the dunlin but are scarce or rare in Ireland and are beyond the scope of this guide.

Snipe *Mionnán Aeir (Meath Gabhar)*

A,W   L=25-27   WS=37-43
Gallinago gallinago (PLATE 5)

MAIN FEATURES About the size of a blackbird. Long straight bill; boldly patterned head and back; barred flanks; pale belly; short stout dark legs; big feet. **In flight**: takes to the air with an explosive zig-zag flight path; thin white stripe on the trailing edge of the wing.

VOICE GUIDE Its call is a short, very harsh, scraping sound, uttered once or repeated when it takes off. Its song, performed from a prominent position in a bog, is a loud, repetitive *tchic-ca*.

GENERAL INFORMATION One of our most common breeding waders, though it has declined in recent years. The snipe is normally very hard to see on the ground, being perfectly camouflaged and preferring to stay in the cover of reeds or rushes. During the winter it can be found in bogs and flooded fields, particularly beet fields, after harvest. It breeds almost anywhere in Ireland where a boggy or marshy habitat is found, but is declining in numbers due to the disappearance of our most threatened habitat for breeding birds – lowland wet grassland. The aerial acrobatics of the display flight include drumming, a muted, rapidly-repeated, humming sound produced by wind rushing through its stiff outer tail feathers held at right angles to its body while diving towards the ground. One of its Irish names is *gabhar* or goat, the sound of which accurately suggests the sound of this drumming.

Irish snipe rarely travel far, except in very cold weather. Local birds are joined by many birds from the Baltic countries, the Faeroes and Iceland.

Curlew *Crotach*

W   L=50-60   WS=80-100
Numenius arquata (PLATE 5)

MAIN FEATURES Largest European wader. *Upper parts*: a complex pattern of browns and buffs; conspicuous white triangle on lower back and rump; tail barred dark brown and white. *Underside*: boldly streaked buff and black; white behind the legs; bill very long and down-curving, dark brown; pink at the base in young birds; legs dark blue-grey. The secondaries, primaries and primary coverts are darker brown than the rest of the wings and back. **In flight**: flocks fly in loose groups, lines or Vs.

VOICE GUIDE One of the noisiest birds on a mudflat, its alarm call often sends every other bird within earshot into the air. Its call is a loud lonely *cuur-lee*. It also makes softer purring noises.

GENERAL INFORMATION It breeds in areas of rough grazing and upland habitat mainly north of a line from Dundalk to Killarney. Numbers have declined recently due mainly to land drainage and afforestation. In winter, birds from northern England, Scotland and northern Europe join our own birds. It can be found anywhere on the island where mud is available under either fresh or salt water. It often feeds on earthworms in grassland. On mud it hunts mainly for worms but shellfish and even crabs will be eaten.

Redshank *Ladhrán Trá*

W   L=27-29   WS=45-52
Tringa totanus (PLATE 5)

MAIN FEATURES Medium-sized wader. **Summer**: brown, heavily streaked and spotted, underside paler. **Winter**: greyer above, less streaked below. Legs long, bright orange-red; bill fairly short and straight, orange-red with a dark tip. **In flight**: broad white trailing edge to dark upper wing and white triangle on the lower back and rump are characteristic.

VOICE GUIDE When disturbed utters a loud harsh repeated *tieuu-ieuu-ieuu*.

GENERAL INFORMATION Breeds in very small numbers in lowland wet grassland, mainly in the northern half of the island with the largest concentration in the west midlands and Connaught. In winter we also get birds from Iceland and northern Britain. It feeds in loose flocks, mainly on small worms and invertebrates found while probing in mud. Usually seen in estuaries.

Turnstone *Piardálaí Trá*

W   L=22-23   WS=46
Arenaria interpres (PLATE 5)

MAIN FEATURES Slightly smaller than a blackbird, short neck and tail. **Winter**: dark grey-brown above with pale edges to the feathers giving a scaled effect; head paler grey-brown, throat white, breast dark brown with paler patches on the side of the breast, giving a rounded W pattern when seen head-on; belly and undertail white. Short dark brown bill, thick at the base and tapering to a fine tip. Short thick bright orange legs. **Summer**: rarely seen in this plumage. Head, neck and breast a complex pattern of black and white, orange marmalade colours on the wings. Female usually duller than the male. **In flight**: upper parts form a striking pattern of browns, black and white. Rarely seen alone. Flies fast and straight, usually low over the water. Often reluctant to fly, preferring to walk or run.

VOICE GUIDE Calls in flight and on the ground. Call notes are variable but include a rapidly repeated *tuck-tuck-tuck* … often rising in pitch and speed towards the end. Lower piping notes are also heard.

GENERAL INFORMATION Can be found anywhere along our coastline from late July to April, with a particular preference for rocky shoreline and stony beaches. As its name suggests it will often be heard turning stones in search of shrimps, sea snails and barnacles. Its diet is very varied and even includes dead fish. It also turns seaweed where it is exposed or on the high tide line. Ringing studies suggest that Irish turnstones come here from their breeding ground in Greenland, stopping off in Iceland on the way to refuel, though some birds probably fly non-stop. When they lose their bright summer plumage they become almost invisible on rocky or seaweed-covered shore. Also seen in estuaries where they will roost on bouys and boats, and occasionally seen on inland lakes. It is estimated that up to 20,000 turnstones spend the winter in Ireland each year. Very small numbers are seen here in summer.

Black-headed
Gull *Faoileán an Chaipín*

W L=38-44 WS=94-105
Larus ridibundus (PLATE 6)

MAIN FEATURES A small gull. **Summer**: wings and back pale grey, white leading edge and black tips to the primaries; head chocolate-brown, not black; rest of body white; legs and bill deep red. **Winter**: same as summer, but head is white with a dark spot behind the eye. **Immature**: brown on the wings; dark band on the end of the tail;

FULMAR
P. 104

GANNET
P. 105 (A)

CORMORANT
P. 106 (S)

SHAG
P.107

BLACK
GUILLEMOT
P. 134 (S)

GUILLEMOT
P. 134 (S)

RAZORBILL
P.135 (S)

KEY.
(A) Adult
(M) Male
(F) Female
(W) Winter
(S) Summer

PLATE 1

MOORHEN
P. 120

LITTLE GREBE
(S) P. 103

SEDGE
WARBLER
P. 157

COOT
P. 120

PLATE 2

GREY HERON
P. 107 (A)

WATER RAIL
P. 118

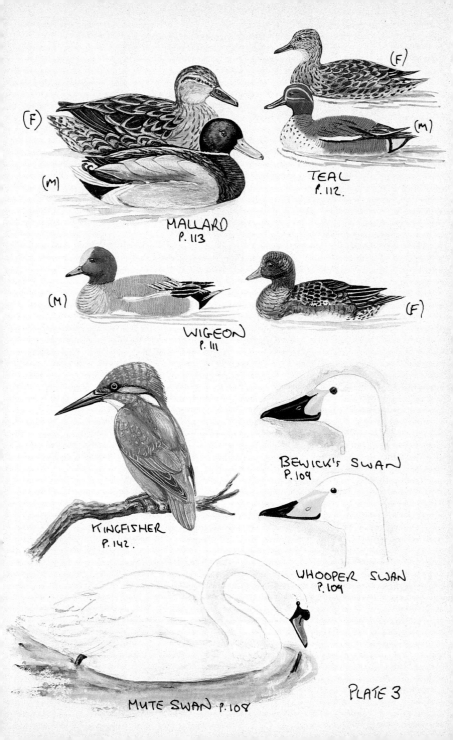

(F)

(F)

(M)

TEAL
P. 112.

(F)

(M)

MALLARD
P. 113

(M)

WIGEON
P. 111

(F)

BEWICK'S SWAN
P. 109

KINGFISHER
P. 142.

WHOOPER SWAN
P. 109

MUTE SWAN P. 108

PLATE 3

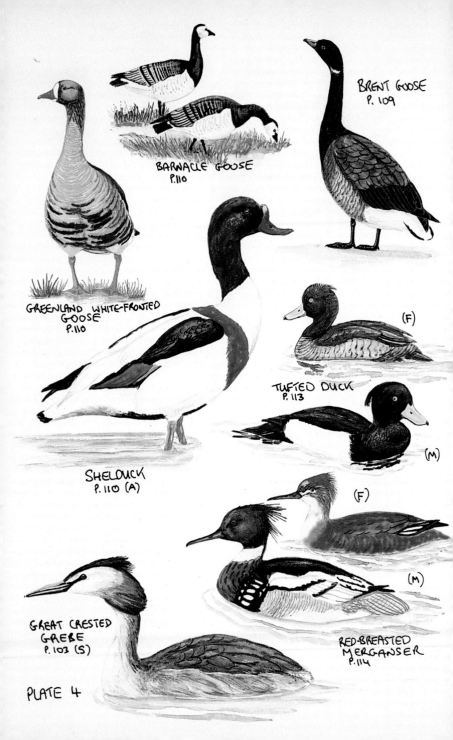

BARNACLE GOOSE
P. 110

BRENT GOOSE
P. 109

GREENLAND WHITE-FRONTED
GOOSE
P. 110

TUFTED DUCK
P. 113

(F)

(M)

SHELDUCK
P. 110 (A)

(F)

(M)

GREAT CRESTED
GREBE
P. 103 (S)

RED-BREASTED
MERGANSER
P. 114

PLATE 4

Oystercatcher
P. 121

Curlew
P. 126

Ringed Plover
P. 122 (s)

Lapwing
P. 123

Redshank
P. 127

Dunlin
P. 124 (s)

Turnstone
P. 127

Snipe
P. 125

Plate 5

(S)

BLACK-HEADED GULL
P. 128 (A)

(W)

HERRING GULL
P. 129 (A)

COMMON GULL
P. 130 (A)

GREAT BLACK-BACKED
GULL
P. 130 (A)

ARCTIC TERN
P. 133 (S)(A)

SANDWICH TERN
P. 131 (S)(A)

COMMON TERN
P. 132 (S)(A)

PLATE 6

WOODPIGEON
P. 135

ROCK DOVE
P. 136

COLLARED
DOVE
P. 137

SKYLARK
P. 143

MEADOW
PIPIT
P. 147

PIED
WAGTAIL
P. 149

STARLING
P. 170 (A)

PLATE 7

BARN OWL
P. 139

SHORT-EARED OWL
P. 141

KESTREL
P. 116

(m)

(M)

LONG-EARED OWL
P. 140

SPARROWHAWK
P. 115

(F)

PEREGRINE
P. 116

PLATE 8

HOUSE MARTIN
P. 146

SAND MARTIN
P. 144

SWIFT
P. 141

SWALLOW
P. 145

(M)

CUCKOO
P. 138

PLATE 9

ROBIN
P. 152

BLACKBIRD
P. 154

(M)

(F)

WREN
P. 151

SONG
THRUSH
P. 155

DUNNOCK
P. 152

PLATE 10

MISTLE THRUSH
P. 156

SPOTTED FLYCATCHER
P. 161

WILLOW WARBLER
P. 159

CHIFFCHAFF
P. 158

(F)

(M)

PHEASANT
P. 117

CORNCRAKE
P. 119

PLATE 11

GOLDCREST
P. 160 (A)

ROCK PIPIT
P. 148

GREY WAGTAIL
P. 149 (M)(S)

DIPPER
P. 150

STONECHAT
P. 153 (M)

PLATE 12

BLUE TIT
P. 163

GREAT TIT
P. 164

COAL TIT
P. 163

LONG-TAILED TIT
P. 162

(M)

(F)

BLACKCAP
P. 158

PLATE 13

MAGPIE
P. 165

JACKDAW
P. 166

RAVEN
P. 169

HOODED CROW
P. 168

ROOK
P. 167 (A)

CHOUGH
P. 168

PLATE 14

CHAFFINCH
P. 172

(F)

(M)

GREENFINCH
P. 173

(M)

(F)

HOUSE SPARROW
P. 171

(F)

(M)

TREE
SPARROW
P. 172

(M)

SISKIN
P. 175

(F)

(M)

(F)

REDPOLL
P. 177

PLATE 15

REED
BUNTING
P. 180 (S)

(M)

(F)

YELLOW HAMMER
P. 179 (S)

(M)

(F)

GOLDFINCH
P. 174

BULLFINCH
P. 178

(M)

(F)

LINNET
P. 176 (S)

(M)

(F)

PLATE 16

legs orange-yellow; bill pale brown-yellow, black tip; identical in size and shape to the adults. **In flight**: pale grey on back and wings; white leading edge to outer primaries forming a long, thin white triangle (above and below) with a black trailing edge. Immatures have dark trailing edge to the secondaries also. Brown on the wing coverts and a dark tail band. Wings very pointed. Will circle and soar in small flocks in vulture-like fashion.

VOICE GUIDE Can be very noisy, especially when feeding. Calls are higher in pitch than the larger gulls, and include a drawn-out *kaaww*, and also a softer chatter, especially when not excited or when washing.

GENERAL INFORMATION It might be surprising to learn that, unlike most other seagulls, it breeds mainly in the midlands, west and north of the country on bogs, marshes, brackish lagoons and islands.

From July onwards, adults and young birds with their noticeable brown markings on the back of the neck and side of the breast begin to appear away from the breeding colonies, especially in estuaries. They are more common on the east and south coasts. By mid-winter it is our most numerous gull and is found all over the country. It is rarely seen on its own and is at home feeding on a mudflat, playing field or refuse tip, behind fishing boats or tractors. It is the most likely gull to visit gardens where it will feed on bread or other kitchen scraps.

The most migratory of our gulls, large numbers of black-headed gulls come here each winter from Britain, Scandinavia and eastern Europe.

Herring Gull *Faoileán Scadán*

A   L=55-67   WS=130-158
Larus argentatus (PLATE 6)

MAIN FEATURES Larger than the black-headed gull. **Adult**: body white, back and wings light grey, black and white wing tips; legs pink; bill yellow with a red spot; eyes yellow. In winter, head and neck can become mottled grey-brown.

Immature: dirty grey-brown head and body; wings a complex pattern of browns, black and buff, primaries and secondaries dark brown; black bill and tail band; gradual plumage change over four years to reach adult plumage. **In flight**: light blue-grey back and wings above with black and white wing tips (much more black than white). Thin white trailing edge to the wing. Immatures have varying amounts of brown on the body and wings, usually with no white at the wing tips. In strong winds will glide on bowed wings high over land and sea.

VOICE GUIDE Calls include a loud repeated *kuwaa* and a laugh-like *agah-ga-ga*.

GENERAL INFORMATION This large gull is found not only all along our coast but also inland, especially in winter. It is a scavenger and so will be found anywhere there is a possibility of a free meal, such as at rubbish dumps, around fishing boats or along the shoreline.

It makes its nest, usually in long grass or under tall weeds, at the top of sea cliffs or on offshore islands. In recent years has taken to nesting on roof-tops in towns and cities, which to it are man-made 'islands'. Herring gulls are very noisy and defend their territory during the breeding season with great energy. They will dive-bomb anything that intrudes, sometimes even hitting it with their bill or wings. Irish herring gulls do not usually travel very far and can live for over 20 years.

CONFUSION SPECIES: *Common Gull* (PLATE 6): smaller. Adult: yellow legs, no red spot on yellow bill, more white on wing tips; high squeaky call. Immature: similar, but never as brown. *Kittiwake* (NOT ILLUSTRATED): smaller. Adult: black wing tips. Immature: black M pattern in the upper parts.

Great Black-backed Gull *Droimneach Mór*

A   L=64-78   WS=150-170
Larus marinus (PLATE 6)

MAIN FEATURES Largest Irish gull. **Adult**: jet-black wings surrounded by a thin white edge;

black back, white body and tail; pink legs and massive yellow bill with a red spot. **Immature**: similar to herring gull, distinguished by larger size and massive black bill. **In flight**: black back and broad black wings with a white trailing and leading edge, white wing tips; strong agile flight.

VOICE GUIDE Calls are deeper than a herring gull's, including a short *ouawk*.

GENERAL INFORMATION The great black-backed gull dominates all other gulls and it is not unusual for it to kill and eat other gulls and auks (especially young birds). It also steals food from other gulls and has a very broad diet.

Not very numerous, and primarily coastal, it often spends a lot of time far out to sea, following fishing boats. It nests on the tops of sea cliffs and offshore islands.

CONFUSION SPECIES *Lesser Black-backed Gull* (not illustrated): smaller, same size as herring gull; dark grey, back and wings not black; bright egg-yolk yellow legs. Immature: similar to herring gulls but darker.

Sandwich Tern *Geabhróg Scothdhubh*

S   L=36-41   WS=98-105
Sterna sandvicensis (PLATE 6)

MAIN FEATURES Largest of our terns, usually advertises its presence with its rasping call. **Adult**: very white-looking; short deeply forked white tail, back and wings very light blue-grey; body white, crown black; characteristic shaggy appearance to the top of the nape; long, dagger-like bill, black with a pale yellow tip. **Immature**: black V-shaped marks on the wings and back. Fed by parents for some time after it has fledged. **In flight**: outer primaries slightly dark and primary tips darker again.

VOICE GUIDE A very noisy tern, uttering a loud grating *kierr-eek* call, often difficult to locate as it has a habit of sometimes flying much higher than other terns.

GENERAL INFORMATION This, the largest of the Irish terns, is the first to reach our shores in mid-March from its wintering grounds in west Africa, and the last to leave in October. Apart from two inland colonies in Mayo and Fermanagh, it also nests at traditional sites on the coast or on off-shore islands, mainly in the north-western half of the country. It was first recorded breeding in Ireland as recently as 1850 on Rockabill Island off the Dublin coast, now the north European stronghold of the rare and endangered roseate tern. The largest colonies are found at Strangford Lough, County Down, where over a thousand pairs breed each year.

Common Tern *Geabhróg*

S   L=31-35   WS=82-95
Sterna hirundo (PLATE 6)

MAIN FEATURES Smaller than the sandwich tern. **Adult**: crown and forehead black in summer, forehead white in winter; body and forked tail white; upper wings pale grey, outer four or five primary tips dark grey-black; legs red; bill short and thin, orange-red with a black tip. **Immature**: white forehead and dark-edged feathers giving a scaled effect to the back and wings, darkest on the leading edge of the inner part of the wing. **In flight**: looks very buoyant on the wing; strong, deep wing beats, glides and circles before diving.

VOICE GUIDE Noisy at the breeding colony. Calls include a drawn-out, descending *keeeeeey*, and high, rapid *kirree-kirree-kirree*.

GENERAL INFORMATION It usually arrives here in late April or early May and departs for its wintering grounds on the west African coast in September. Referred to by sailors as the sea-swallow because of its long forked tail. Feeds mainly on sand eels and sprats which it catches by plunging head first into the water and flying off immediately. Like all terns it rarely lands on water, preferring beaches, rocky shores, small islands, moored boats and buoys.

It breeds in colonies around our coast and on inland lakes, such as on the Shannon, Lough Erne and Lough Neagh. It is our most widely-distributed breeding tern and at times shows an unusual tolerance of man, nesting on barges, rafts and undisturbed docklands. Numbers have been declining here in recent years and there is a noticeable northward shift in their breeding range.

A common tern ringed on Copeland Island, County Down, in May 1959 was found in Victoria, Australia, in October 1968, over 17,000 kilometres away.

CONFUSION SPECIES *Arctic Tern* (PLATE 6): see below.

Arctic Tern *Geabhróg Artach*

S   L=33-35   WS=80-95
Sterna paradisaea (PLATE 6)

MAIN FEATURES Very similar to the common tern but with greyer wings, darker all-red bill, shorter legs and longer tail. **In flight**: looks paler than common tern, especially the wings.

VOICE GUIDE Similar to common tern but also an upward whistling *kee-kee*.

GENERAL INFORMATION Considered to be the creature that sees most daylight. As its name suggests, some nest inside the Arctic Circle in summer and unlike the very similar-looking common tern, they winter near the pack ice of Antarctica.

Prefers coastal nesting sites and rarely seen inland. Usually more aggressive than common terns and will attack any intruders to the nesting colony by dive-bombing, drawing blood from unprotected heads with its sharp bill.

Guillemot *Muiréan*

A L=38-45 WS=64-73

Uria aalga (PLATE I)

MAIN FEATURES Summer: chocolate-brown upper parts, head, throat and breast, white belly; white tips to secondaries forming a narrow white trailing edge to the inner wing. A very small percentage of guillemots have a thin white eye ring and eye stripe extending back from the eye like a monocle. Legs black, very short and set far back on the body; the feet are webbed. **Winter**: plumage the same, except throat, neck and breast become white; long down-curving narrow black eye stripe extends back from the eye. **In flight**: moves very fast, rapid 'whirring' wing beats; usually travels in small groups.

VOICE GUIDE Very noisy at breeding colonies. Its loud, slightly muted, drawn-out *ooaarrrrr* is easily heard above the din of other breeding seabirds. Usually silent outside the breeding season.

GENERAL INFORMATION Our most common auk, nesting on steep cliff ledges and sea-stacks around our coast. It nests in large noisy colonies. In the early 1970s half of all the guillemots breeding in Ireland were found at just three colonies, Rathlin Island in Antrim, Lambay Island in Dublin and Great Saltee Island in Wexford. It usually lays just one egg and when hatched the young are often formed into crêches, with one parent minding a few chicks while the others go fishing. In winter it leaves the breeding cliffs, young birds usually travelling farther than adults and, though usually seen on the sea, can occasionally be found in estuaries, or further inland after gales. It feeds on fish which it catches by diving from the surface of the water, using its stiff narrow wings to 'fly' underwater in search of food. Away from breeding colonies, best seen in spring and autumn from headlands.

CONFUSION SPECIES *Razorbill* (PLATE I): see below. *Black Guillemot* (PLATE I): in summer all black with large white wing patches; in winter much paler than guillemot; wing patches noticeable in flight.

Razorbill *Crosán*

A L=37-39   WS=63-67
Alca torda (PLATE 1)

MAIN FEATURES Distinguished from the guillemot by much heavier, blunt bill with white crescent on the outer half. Thin white line running from the eye to the base of the bill. Shorter thicker neck, bigger head and the upper parts are black rather than chocolate brown. Summer and winter plumages similar to guillemot.

VOICE GUIDE Whistles and long growls at the breeding colony.

GENERAL INFORMATION At a distance in flight or on the sea almost indistinguishable from guillemots to all except the most experienced of bird watchers. It also shares similar summer and winter habits and distribution with the more common guillemots. Along with other members of the auk family, razorbills are the birds most often killed in oil slicks because, while hunting, they will often resurface under the enveloping blanket of oil.

CONFUSION SPECIES *Guillemot* (PLATE 1): see above.

Woodpigeon *Colm Coille**

A   L=40-42   WS=75-80
Columba palumbus (PLATE 7)

MAIN FEATURES Adult: pure white neck patches and wing crescents on the wings; pink-grey breast, rest of body greyer; rump and lower back pale blue-grey; tail dark above, more clearly marked grey and black below; very fat-looking; small head; short red legs; pale yellow and pink bill; pale cream iris. **Immature**: as adult, but lacks white on the neck. **In flight**: when flying out of trees it can make a loud racket as its wings hit leaves and branches. Its display flight, used to defend its territory, involves a steep flight upwards ending in loud wing claps and a downward glide, sometimes repeated.

VOICE GUIDE Call is a series of loud cooing notes sounding like *Take two, John, take two*. This phrase is often repeated several times and may start in the middle of one.

GENERAL COMMENTS As the name suggests, woodpigeons usually nest in trees and bushes but will also nest in any safe areas, even on the ground in some places. Not usually migratory, with very small numbers coming here from Britain and mainland Europe.

Feeds on seeds, berries, buds, beechmast (beechnuts), and acorns. Can do serious damage to crops, especially during the winter, when it will feed on kale, turnips, and clover. The recent increase in the planting of oilseed rape has turned this pigeon into a serious 'pest'. It will also visit vegetable patches early in the morning and can clean out a whole bed of newly-emerging plants very quickly without being seen. In autumn, flocks of up to 15,000 have been seen and with so much food available survival rates for young is very high. It has been conservatively estimated that as many as three million woodpigeons are in Ireland each autumn.

CONFUSION SPECIES *Stock Dove* (NOT ILLUSTRATED): slightly smaller, darker, with no white areas on neck or wings. *Rock Dove* (PLATE 7): similar to stock dove but with large white rump patch; found on remote sea cliffs in the west. *Feral Pigeon* (NOT ILLUSTRATED): also called a racing pigeon, comes in all patterns and colours from almost all black to pure white or rusty red. Found mainly in urban areas. True racing pigeons will have one or two rings on the legs.

Collared Dove *Fearán Baicdhubh*

A L=31-33 WS=47-55
Streptopelia decaocto (PLATE7)

MAIN FEATURES Slim, sand-coloured dove. *Upper parts*: brown back and inner wing, dark brown-black outer primaries. *Underside*: pale grey-brown underside, distinctive but not always noticeable black half-collar at base of the neck; bill short, thin and dark; eyes dark red; legs short and powdery pink. **In flight**: flies straight with fast jerky wing beats. In display flight it glides with stiff, slightly down-curved wings and fanned tail, clearly showing the pale under-wing and white undertail with a black band at the base.

VOICE GUIDE Its call is a gentle 'cooing' sound phrased like *can yoouuu coo* repeated two or more times.

GENERAL COMMENTS The collared dove is a recent colonist in Ireland. In 1930 the nearest breeding birds were in Yugoslavia. Following the most amazing population explosion, 29 years later it was breeding over most of Europe and reached Ireland in 1959 when it was first recorded in counties Down, Dublin and Galway. It first bred in counties Kildare, Kilkenny and Louth as recently as 1969. Now it is estimated that as many as 30,000 pairs breed in Ireland.

It dislikes high ground and open countryside and nests on or close to buildings. Its diet is made up mainly of cereal grains but it will also eat weed seeds and insects. It has even become a regular visitor to bird tables, but remains very wary. Often perches on overhead wires and lamp posts.

Cuckoo *Cuach*

S   L=32-34   WS=55-65
Cuculus canorus (PLATE 9)

MAIN FEATURES Male: upper parts grey with grey-brown primaries and secondaries; tail grey-brown with white tips to the tail feathers; throat and breast grey; belly boldly barred black and white; bill short, thin, black with a yellow base; legs short and yellow. **Female**: browner, especially on the breast. **Immature**: darker above and scaled-looking. **In flight**: resembles a hawk with long pointed wings and a long round-ended tail. Fast fluttering flight, wings never raised above the body. Usually glides briefly before landing.

VOICE GUIDE No need to describe the call of the male which gives this well-known bird its name. The female makes a high bubbling sound.

GENERAL INFORMATION The cuckoo arrives in Ireland from its African wintering grounds in the second half of April. It lays its eggs in the nests of other birds, usually meadow pipits, but also other insect-eating birds such as the dunnock and the sedge warbler. When the young hatch they immediately evict all other eggs and young so that there will be no competition for all the food brought by its foster-parents. The young cuckoo grows fast and soon outgrows the tiny nest. The foster-parents are soon over-shadowed by the giant chick and even have to stand on its back to feed it. Cuckoos are insect-eaters and love hairy caterpillars which are usually avoided by other birds. The adults leave Ireland before the young in early August, the young following unaided in late August and early September.

CONFUSION SPECIES *Sparrowhawk* (PLATE 8): very round-ended, not pointed, wings.

Barn Owl *Scréachóg Reilige*

A L=37-39 WS=85-93

Tyto alba (PLATE 8)

MAIN FEATURES About the size of a jackdaw. Flat, white, heart-shaped face with large black eyes; upper parts deep yellow-buff with small dark flecks; underside white; legs long with large taloned feet; looks 'knock-kneed' when perched; no ear tufts. **In flight**: silent, blunt head; short tail; wings broad and round-tipped; wing beats jerky and stiff.

VOICE GUIDE The quietest of our owls but occasionally makes a loud shriek. The young make a hissing noise. The hooting call sometimes attributed to the barn owl and heard on television and radio is made by the tawny owl, a species common in Britain, but which does not occur in Ireland.

GENERAL COMMENTS Ireland's most well-known, yet threatened, owl, it is usually seen briefly in the light of a car or a street lamp. A largely nocturnal bird, it rarely hunts by day and is the source of many a 'ghost-sighting'. The best chance of seeing one is either in the headlights of a car at night or at dawn or dusk during the breeding season. Sometimes killed by cars and found dead by the roadside.

In Ireland many keen birdwatchers may only see one or two barn owls in a year. Its numbers have declined in recent years through a combination of a decrease in suitable nest sites, intensification of farming, and the use of rodenticides. It is more numerous in the south-eastern half of the country.

It usually eats wood mice and pygmy shrews, and in urban areas it appears that its diet includes an increased proportion of small birds, house mice and rats. Bank voles, where they occur, form 20 percent to 25 percent of their prey items.

It usually eats wood mice and pygmy shrews, and in urban areas it appears that its diet includes an increased proportion of small birds, house mice and rats. Bank voles, where they occur, form 20 percent to 25 percent of their prey items.

Long-eared Owl *Ceann Cait*

A   L=35-47   WS=84-95
Asio otus (PLATE 8)

MAIN FEATURES Roughly the same size as the barn owl. Upper parts a complex pattern of light and dark browns, grey, and some white spots on the inner wing area; underside light brown with heavy dark streaking; eyes fiery red-orange; feather tufts that look like ears. **In flight**: very stiff, jerky flight; indistinct dark patch on the leading edge of the outer wing.

VOICE GUIDE Like most owls usually silent but during the breeding season the male makes a low moaning *whoo–oooo–oooo* call, also makes squeaks and clapping sounds.

GENERAL INFORMATION Our most common owl and yet probably not seen as often as the barn owl. It occurs wherever there are small stands of trees with open countryside nearby. It has also become associated with forestry plantations and appears to be increasing in numbers. Feeds mainly on wood mice and rats. Small numbers migrate here from the continent each winter.

CONFUSION SPECIES *Short-eared Owl* (PLATE 8): see below.

Short-eared Owl *Ulchabhán Réisc*

W (scarce)   L=34-42   WS=90-105
Asio flammeus (PLATE 8)

MAIN FEATURES Generally paler than the long-eared owl; conspicuous pale yellow patch high-lighting a dark patch at the bend of the upper wing, most noticeable in flight. The rest of the upper parts is a complex pattern of dark-brown, white and buff. Short tail barred dark-brown and white; eyes yellow, surrounded by dark 'shadows'; very small 'ear' tufts.

VOICE GUIDE The males make a low repeating *boo-boo-boo-boo*, females a high short *keee-aw*.

GENERAL INFORMATION The rarest of our owls, mainly a winter visitor, with only a few breeding records. Unlike our other owls, the short-eared owl hunts in the early morning and late in the evening and prefers large open spaces. Usually seen on open coastal areas or over large bogs, gliding with great expertise in search of mice or rats. Rarely seen in tall trees, preferring to perch on the ground, a low bush or post. Most sightings are away from the west coast.

CONFUSION SPECIES *Long-eared Owl* (PLATE 8): see above.

Swift *Gabhlán Gaoithe*

S   L=16-17   WS=42-48
Apus apus (PLATE 9)

MAIN FEATURES Almost completely aerial existence. **In flight**: all black plumage, except for a pale throat, visible only at close range; long, scythe-shaped wings; stiff wing beats thought by some to alternate; short, forked tail which can look pointed. Swifts often gather at dusk in large noisy groups, high in the sky, sometimes heard but not seen.

VOICE GUIDE A distinct sound of summer is a group of swifts, screaming with high-pitched buzzing calls, speeding low over houses and streets.

GENERAL INFORMATION Of our summer visitors it is one of the latest to arrive and the earliest to depart, coming at the beginning of May and leaving in August. Usually associated with population centres of all sizes, where it nests under the eaves of buildings, the taller the better. Lands only to rear young and even sleeps on the wing. As a result of this aerial existence, if a swift becomes grounded it is usually unable to take off again and moves with difficulty on the ground.

It feeds on insects which it catches by flying quickly with its mouth wide open. Its name is slightly misleading because even a robin can fly faster than this bird at top speed. When feeding young, the insects are stored in a ball in the crop or throat pouch. It travels far to find food and so can be seen almost anywhere, though scarcer in the west.

Kingfisher *Cruidín*

A   L=16-17   WS=24-26
Alcedo atthis (PLATE 3)

MAIN FEATURES Short rounded sky-blue wings with white spots on the inner half; brilliant metallic light-blue back; breast, belly and ear coverts red-orange; throat and a patch directly behind the ear coverts white; long, dark dagger-shaped bill; female has red-orange on the lower mandible; very short red legs. Can be difficult to locate when perched. **In flight**: low, straight buzzing flight with occasional gliding. Often noticed only when it darts along a river or across a lake.

VOICE GUIDE Its call is a very loud, piercing *pseeeeee* often repeated several times, usually in flight.

GENERAL INFORMATION Show people a painting or photograph of this bird and 99 percent will identify it correctly, yet very few will ever have seen one. One of our most colourful birds, the kingfisher is only slightly bigger than a robin, an impression not gained by the fabulous close-up and enlarged photographs that regularly appear in books and magazines. Prefers ponds, lakes and slow-moving streams. It will sit on favourite branches and posts, from where it plunge-dives onto small fish just below the surface of the water, returning to its perch to beat its catch off the wood before swallowing it head first. When feeding young, it will fly off with the fish tail first in its bill.

More common in the eastern half of the country. After the breeding season many move to the coast and can be found almost anywhere, from remote bays to city-centre docklands. Unlike Continental European populations which decline dramatically after very cold winters when food is unavailable, numbers here do not vary as dramatically. There has recently been a population decline in this tropical-looking bird mainly due to river pollution, disturbance by humans during the breeding season and the removal of steep river banks in which it excavates its nest hole.

Skylark *Fuiseóg* *

A L=18-19
Alauda arvensis (PLATE 7)

MAIN FEATURES *Upper parts*: sandy brown, streaked with dark brown; white outer tail feathers; thin white trailing edge to wing, visible only when open; characteristic short broad crest, though not always raised. *Underside*: white belly; buff breast with dark streaking, heaviest at the sides; bill pale, short and stubby; legs long, pale pink with a very long claw on the hind toe. **In flight**: if disturbed from the ground usually flutters a short distance before landing in long grass and will usually run off. Long flights undulating, with the wings completely closed on the downward glide.

VOICE GUIDE One of the first birds to be heard in the morning in open countryside, its almost continuous song consists of an energetic jumble of twittering, chirping, warbling sounds often including imitations of other species. It sings as it rises and hovers on fluttering wings, sometimes until it is almost out of sight. Its call is a loud thin *chirrup*.

GENERAL INFORMATION Over one million skylarks breed in Ireland each year. This makes it a very common bird indeed, especially in open country and on coastal dunes. It nests on the ground usually under a clump of tall grass. It often perches (and sings) on fence posts. In the winter large flocks can be seen, especially over stubble fields where, almost unnoticed on the ground, they eat cereal grain and insects.

Sand Martin *Gamhlán Gainimh*

S L=12

Riparia riparia (PLATE 9)

MAIN FEATURES Adult: upper parts dark brown; creamy white body below; inconspicuous dark brown breast band. **Immature**: similar; upper parts have scaled appearance; underside buffer. **In flight**: wings all dark, pointed; tail short and forked. Draws wings close to body in erratic flight with occasional glides.

VOICE GUIDE Calls include a short *brrtt*, and a sharp *tcheerup*. Its song is a collection of weak twittering notes.

GENERAL INFORMATION The sand martin arrives in Ireland in late March from its wintering ground in Africa, south of the Sahara. Its name gives us a clue to its favourite breeding habitat, that is sand cliffs, especially sand and gravel pits, though it has been recorded using other nest sites and has even been known to use turf banks. Nests in holes which it makes in the cliff, usually near the top. Undoubtedly their numbers have increased as more pits are opened. Its population fluctuates a lot because it is very susceptible to drought in its wintering grounds. It often rears two broods of young, the first brood heading south as early as late July.

Feeds on insects and spiders which it catches in flight, often over water. In autumn, gathers in large groups on the coast before migrating south along the shores of western Europe.

CONFUSION SPECIES *House Martin* (PLATE 9): black and white with an obvious white rump patch. *Swallow* (PLATE 9): blue-black above; longer, forked tail, deep red-brown throat.

Swallow *Fáinleóg* *

S   L=19-22
Hirundo rustica (PLATE 9)

MAIN FEATURES *Upper parts*: blue-black with a blue metallic sheen on the back and head. *Under-side*: forehead and throat red-brown, paler on young birds; black breast band; white or cream belly and under tail; long outer tail feathers, longer in the males than the females or young; white spots forming a crescent near the end of the tail, most noticeable from below; tiny, slightly hooked black bill; very short black legs. **In flight**: an agile flyer, dips, dives and glides.

VOICE GUIDE The call is a short *whit* sound. The song is a series of fast twittering sounds interspersed with chattering and whistling notes.

GENERAL INFORMATION Even though it is said that it takes more than one swallow to make a summer, its arrival always sparks off conversation about how good or bad our summer will be. Proof that there are far more birdwatchers in Ireland than you think!

A bird of the countryside, rarely seen in the centre of cities or towns. It makes its half-cup nest of mud on rafters and walls in barns and outhouses, and it has also been recorded nesting in caves.

Catches insects on the wing and favours large flies such as bluebottles, hoverflies and horseflies, catching thousands each summer. It rears up to three broods with four or five young per brood. In August and September it gathers in large flocks on the coast, usually over reed beds where up to 30,000 birds have been counted on occasions. It winters in southern Africa. There has been a slight decline in recent years and pesticides and modern farm design (no more gaps at the top of barn doors) may be the cause.

House Martin *Gabhlán Binne*

S L=12-13
Delichon urbica (PLATE 9)

MAIN FEATURES Smaller than the swallow. Upper parts black with metallic blue sheen; obvious square white rump patch; short black forked tail; underside white; very short white feet. **In flight**: agile, flutters and glides; black and white appearance; white rump patch.

VOICE GUIDE Call a loud clear *prreet*, usually heard near the colony.

GENERAL INFORMATION Another summer visitor that feeds on the wing, more common in the eastern half of the island. Its preference for nesting under the eaves of houses explains its name. Like the swift it can be found nesting even in the centre of towns and villages. Its nest is made from mud collected from pool edges, shaped into a ball and cemented to the nest wall with saliva. The same nest can be used for several years, with ongoing repairs. The nest is more enclosed than that of the swallow and occasionally house sparrows will take over the nest. Will also nest on suitable coastal cliffs. Colonies range in size from a few nests to over a hundred. Arrives in late April and early May and departs for Africa again in September and October.

CONFUSION SPECIES *Sand Martin* (PLATE 9): browner; dark breast band; all dark above. *Swallow* (PLATE 9): also all dark above, except for small white spots on the tail; red-brown throat; black breast-band.

Meadow Pipit *Riabhóg Mhóna* *

A   L=14-15
Anthus pratensis (PLATE 7)

MAIN FEATURES Same size as a robin, but slimmer in shape. Superficially resembles a miniature thrush. *Upper parts*: head dull brown; back streaked black and brown; tail long and thin; white outer tail feathers. *Underside*: pale buff throat, black streaking on the breast, flanks and upper belly; short fine bill and long pink legs. **In flight**: slightly bouncing flight; white outer tail feathers usually visible as it takes off.

VOICE GUIDE Its call is a high sharp *weeep*, loudest when disturbed or alarmed. Its song is complex, starting with speeding up, high *seep* notes and ending with a melodious trill. Usually sung while rising from the ground and ends with the bird dropping with tail raised in parachute fashion.

GENERAL INFORMATION Like the skylark, the meadow pipit is a ground-loving bird and is one of our most abundant and widespread species. Usually seen singly or in small loose flocks though large flocks are not rare. It feeds on insects. Very common on the western seaboard and least common in the south-east. Nests from the coast to mountain areas, preferring rough pasture and long grass. Changes in land use may explain the lower breeding numbers in the south east. The cuckoo will sometimes lay its eggs in the nests of unsuspecting meadow pipits.

In winter, numbers increase in the south and on low ground, and are more noticeable on the coast. Some even visit gardens. Some Irish meadow pipits migrate to southern Europe and those that remain in Ireland are joined by birds from Continental Europe. Beware of possible confusion with the next species, as they can sometimes be seen feeding side-by-side on the tide-line (usually in the winter).

CONFUSION SPECIES *Rock Pipit* (PLATE 12): see below.

Rock Pipit *Riabhóg Chladaigh*

A   L=17
Anthus petrosus (PLATE 12)

MAIN FEATURES Like a duller, smoky version of its close relative the meadow pipit. Streaking on the back is almost absent; greyer below; outer tail feathers grey, not white; legs dark brown. Bigger than meadow pipit. **In flight**: undulating, dull and featureless with a long tail, grey outer tail feathers not very noticeable.

VOICE GUIDE Call a thin *tweep*, thinner than meadow pipit. Song very similar to meadow pipit, though less musical.

GENERAL INFORMATION Just like the meadow pipit, its name clearly indicates its favoured habitat, rocky sea shores. Found almost all around Ireland, the only gaps being where sand replaces rock-and-gravel shoreline. Nests among rocks usually close to the high-tide line and will raise two broods. Like the last species, the cuckoo also lays it eggs in the nests of rock pipits. Rarely travels far and will defend its territory all year round. Rarely seen away from the coast.

CONFUSION SPECIES *Meadow Pipit* (PLATE 7): smaller, much brighter and more boldly marked, white outer tail feathers.

Grey Wagtail *Glasóg Cheannliath*

A   L=18-19

Motacilla cinerea (PLATE 12)

MAIN FEATURES Male: grey head, mantle and back; thin white supercilium (eyebrow); yellow rump; tail as long as its body, black with white outer feathers; black chin and throat in summer; breast, belly and undertail coverts yellow. **Female**: resembles male but has a white throat and belly; yellow breast and undertail. **In flight**: undulates; noticeable white wing bar and white outer tail feathers.

VOICE GUIDE The call is a loud *zeet-eet*, made when disturbed or in characteristic undulating flight.

GENERAL INFORMATION It is found all over Ireland and is never seen far from water. During the breeding season it prefers fast-flowing rivers and streams, especially when bordered with broad-leaved trees. In the winter it is more numerous in the south-east of the island and can be seen on the coast and anywhere near water. It feeds on insects, mainly flies, which it catches by flying out from its perch to grab the insect with a flurry of wings and a spread tail showing clearly the white outer tail feathers.

Pied Wagtail

(Willy Wagtail) *Siubháinín an Bhóthair*

A   L=18

Mottacilla alba (PLATE 7)

MAIN FEATURES Black and white. **Male**: upper parts black, except for two white wing bars; white face; black forehead and throat; black bib on the breast; belly and undertail coverts white; flanks dark grey; long black and white tail, wagged frequently. **Female** and **imma**ture: grey mantle, back and upper wing coverts. In flight: undulating, short bursts of wing beats followed by dipping glides with wings closed. Black and white.

VOICE GUIDE Call is an explosive, high *tchizzik*. Song similar to the call notes but longer and twittering.

GENERAL INFORMATION A very common bird in Ireland often referred to as the 'willy wagtail'. This bird is at home in the centre of cities or on open bogland. It is an insect-eater and often nests near water. Sometimes seen removing dead insects from wing mirrors and radiator grilles of cars, and has even been known to nest in cars. In the winter, roosts in large flocks in trees and ruins or on flat roof-tops of buildings. In large towns and cities these roosts often contain hundreds of birds.

Dipper *Lon Abhann*

A   L=18
Cinclus cinclus (PLATE 12)
MAIN FEATURES Unmistakeable with its dark plumage, brilliant white throat and breast – at close range the area just below the white breast is dark chestnut; short stumpy tail; short straight black bill; fairly long, stout black legs. **In flight**: fast and straight, continuous rapid wing beats.

VOICE GUIDE Usually short, loud, harsh *tsit*.

GENERAL INFORMATION If it is not seen in flight it is usually perched on a rock in a river or stream. It catches its food in a unique way, by diving underwater and walking along the bottom in search of insect larvae or fish eggs. It pops up again and will sometimes swim or emerge onto a rock. Does not migrate in Ireland and is rarest in the midlands. There is evidence from Wales to suggest that extensive planting of conifers has led to increased acidification of some rivers and streams which, in turn, has led to a decrease in dipper numbers there. There is no proof of this in Ireland to date.

Wren *Dreoilín* *

A L=9-10

Troglodytes troglodytes (PLATE 10)

MAIN FEATURES A tiny rusty-brown bird; paler below; pale supercilium; short rounded wings; fairly long, thin down-curved bill; long thin brown legs. Often cocks its tail so high it almost touches the back of its head. **In flight**: low, straight buzzing flight.

VOICE GUIDE The song is very loud, high and energetic. It has a variety of calls, the most noticeable being a loud short *tchic*, often repeated many times in an irregular, mechanical fashion. Cocks its tail when singing.

GENERAL INFORMATION The third smallest bird in Europe after the goldcrest and firecrest, it would definitely qualify as one of the noisiest. Indeed, if you had never seen one before you would be forgiven for expecting it to be much bigger from the noise it makes. Its Latin name when translated means 'cave-dweller', which aptly describes its behaviour as it spends most of its time deep inside hedges, bushes and undergrowth. Also its ball-shaped nest has a hole on the side and during the breeding season usually contains five or six eggs, though up to 15 have been recorded. With an average life span of less than two years, nature ensures its survival by providing many young. It is estimated that five million wrens breed in Ireland each year, nesting in hedges, stone walls, cliffs, bogs and even old teapots. It feeds mainly on insects and spiders which it hunts in dense undergrowth, usually venturing out only to burst into song from an exposed site. Being so small, wrens die in large numbers during very cold weather and indeed they are less common in more exposed areas of the west of the country during the winter months. Often seen skulking low down in hedges, and in winter some wrens move into reed beds.

Dunnock

(Hedge Sparrow) *Bráthair an Dreoilín* *

A L=14-15
Prunella modularis (PLATE 10)

MAIN FEATURES Upper parts dark brown,
streaked black; underside dark grey, paler
toward undertail coverts; dark streaking on
the flanks; eyes deep red or brown; bill short,
thin and black; legs long, thin and dark brown. When feeding hops along open
ground, usually under bushes, comes to bird tables. **In flight**: slightly undulating but not very fast. No noticeable features.

VOICE GUIDE Call is a high thin *seeep*. The song is wren-like though not as
loud or as long.

GENERAL INFORMATION There are nearly one million breeding pairs in
Ireland. Dunnocks have a very complex social system, sometimes involving two males feeding the one brood of young or one male rearing young
of more than one female. In the winter hedges become very important
for both food and shelter. A largely sedentary bird which rarely travels
far. It is common everywhere except in some parts of the north and
extreme west.

Robin *Spideóg* *

A L=14
Erithacus rubecula (PLATE 10)

MAIN FEATURES **Adult**: bright red-orange
breast; white belly; warm brown upper
parts; grey on the side of the neck and upper
breast; stands upright; round appearance.
Immature: young birds, just out of the nest

do not have a red breast, but instead are scaled light and dark brown. **In flight**: flies fast and straight.

VOICE GUIDE Its call is a loud, thin *ptic*, usually repeated several times, often out of sight. It sings all year round but is at its loudest during spring, when its melodious twittering is often performed from a fence-post or a prominent bush.

GENERAL INFORMATION Probably the best-known bird species in Ireland and also the 'friendliest'. Should not be confused with any other Irish bird. In the breeding season these birds are very territorial and will chase off any intruding robins. Occasionally disputes between neighbouring birds can become very violent. Nests anywhere there is ground cover and will some-times use garden sheds. It can rear up to three broods of young a year. In winter it is a constant companion to the gardener, feeding on grubs, worms and insects disturbed by the fork or spade, and can become very tame. It is the most widespread visitor to bird tables.

Stonechat *Caislín Dearg*

A   L=12-13
Saxicola torquata (PLATE 12)

MAIN FEATURES Male: black head; white patches on the side of the neck and on the wings; bright orange breast and flanks; back streaked dark brown and black; creamy white rump; short black tail; legs long and black; in winter duller and paler. **Female**: paler brown version of the male; no white; less striking orange-brown breast, and lacks pale rump. **In flight**: makes short flights to catch flies and pounce on insects from a prominent position; straight, weak, buzzing flight. Hops on the ground.

VOICE GUIDE It gets its name from its call which is a loud short *tchack-tchack* (like two stones being banged together), sometimes preceded by a longer thin *weeet* sound and accompanied by wing- and tail-flicking. The song is an unremarkable, often double-noted, twittering.

GENERAL INFORMATION It is a sedentary species. Nests in thick vegetation and has a preference for areas of gorse and young forestry plantations. Most abundant along the west coast, it has declined in recent years due to intensive farming and increased human disturbance due to recreational activities. This decline is most noticeable in the east and midlands. Retreats from higher ground in the winter and is mainly found along the coasts. Very sensitive to cold weather when large numbers die, but following a few mild winters and because of their ability to raise three broods of young in a season their numbers soon recover.

Blackbird *Lon Dubh* *

A   L=24-25
Turdus merula (PLATE 10)

MAIN FEATURES Male: jet-black; short, heavy bright orange-yellow bill and eye-ring. **Female**: dark, chocolate-brown, with paler throat and breast (sometimes faintly spotted); dark-brown bill; no eye-ring. Young males superficially resemble females. Partly or total albino blackbirds sometimes seen. **In flight**: over short distances, fast and straight flight. On landing will often droop its wings and cock its tail high in the air.

VOICE GUIDE Sings from a high prominent position, from late January well into summer. The song is melodious and loud, sometimes continuing for a long period. Calls include a loud *chack* and a high pitched, thin *sseeee*. If disturbed flies away with a loud clamouring exclamation.

GENERAL INFORMATION Likes open, short grass and leaf litter where it feeds on worms, snails and insects. Also feeds on fruit and berries. If frightened on the ground it will sometimes lower its head and run quickly to the nearest cover.

With nearly two million breeding pairs in Ireland, it is no wonder that it is so well-known. It is common everywhere but was rare in the west in the last century. Its dark plumage and low-pitched voice has led researchers to believe that the blackbird was once a mainly forest species, before man began changing the landscape in Europe. A ground-feeding bird, it will often be seen looking and listening for earthworms on or just below the surface of the ground. In winter, many blackbirds from Britain and Scandinavia join our mainly resident birds.

Song Thrush *Smólach* *

A L=23
Turdus philomelos (PLATE 10)

MAIN FEATURES Upper parts warm brown; underside pale buff with conspicuous black spots, arranged so close together as to form lines, thinnest on the throat and upper breast, thickest with largest spots on the flanks and belly; eyes black; bill small and sharp, looks up-tilted; legs long and pink. **In flight**: pale buff-orange underwing. Slightly smaller and less robust than the blackbird. On open ground often makes short dashes.

VOICE GUIDE Its call is a loud *thick*, repeated several times quickly. The song, delivered from a high perch, roof or TV aerial, is similar to that of a blackbird, but more musical and structured, containing short phrases repeated clearly two to four times.

GENERAL INFORMATION During 1988-91 there were up to 400,000 breeding pairs in Ireland. It is slightly less common near the coast than inland. Its nest is unusual because it is lined with smooth mud or rotten wood pulp. Like other thrushes, it likes earthworms and can be seen feeding on large lawns and parks. It also likes snails which it smashes open on a favourite small rock or tree stump, often referred to as an anvil, leaving a large number of broken shells. In Britain an alarming increase in the use of snail-killing chemicals in recent years, both commercially and domestically, is thought to be the main cause of a recent decline there. Like the blackbird, song thrushes from Britain and Scandinavia come here each winter, and in severe cold winters thrushes from all over the Continent arrive here in large numbers.

CONFUSION SPECIES *Redwing* (NOT ILLUSTRATED): slightly smaller; pale buff supercilium; red-orange on underwings and flanks; call a thin *tseeep* often heard at night in late autumn and winter. *Mistle Thrush* (PLATE 10): see below.

Mistle Thrush *Smólach Mór*

A L=27

Turdus viscivorus (PLATE 10)

MAIN FEATURES Larger than song thrush. Upper parts dusty grey-brown; wing feathers pale fringed; underside white with fine streaks and blotches on the throat and breast; belly has large distinct dark spots, not forming lines. **In flight**: white underwing; very undulating flight, glides with wings closed. On the ground it stands very erect and looks pot-bellied.

VOICE GUIDE Call is a distinctive rapid, harsh chattering *tuck-tuck-tuck*, often heard when in flight. Its song is similar but less musical and more repetitive than a blackbird.

GENERAL INFORMATION It breeds in all parts of Ireland, though more scarce on the south coast, particularly in County Cork. Unknown in Ireland up to 1800 when one was shot in County Antrim. By the end of the 19th century it was breeding in every county. The reasons for this colonisation are unknown. In the breeding season it feeds its young mainly on caterpillars and flies. In the winter it defends a feeding territory, especially a berry bush or tree, with a particular fondness for holly trees. On the Continent it defends large areas of mistletoe, from which it gets its name. Less migratory than other thrushes, our own birds are sedentary and are joined by small numbers from Britain in the winter.

CONFUSION SPECIES *Song Thrush* (PLATE 10): much smaller, with warmer colours; does not look so spotted (see above).

Sedge Warbler *Ceolaire Cíbe*

S L=13

Acrocephalus schoenobaenus (PLATE 2)

MAIN FEATURES A small bird. Upper parts buff-brown back with dark streaks; dark wings; red-brown rump; short dark tail; pale buff supercilium (eyebrow), dark eye-stripe and crown; underside cream with buff flanks.

Young have fine dark streaks on the side of the breast. Usually heard more often than seen. **In flight**: will sometimes flutter a short distance with tail dipped, while singing.

VOICE GUIDE Its song is a long series of jumbled musical phrases, interspersed with a rattling *tchurr*, and includes the mimicked sounds of other birds. Usually sings near the top of a reed stem or the top of a bush. Its call is a short *tchak*.

GENERAL INFORMATION This summer visitor to Ireland is usually associated with reed beds, but will also be found along wet ditches, ponds and bogs near dense undergrowth. Up to 110,000 pairs of sedge warblers come here each summer from west Africa. Nests close to the ground, in habitat usually containing reeds and low scrub. Mainly coastal in distribution in the south, and most abundant and widespread in the northern half of the country. Has declined in recent years, probably due to habitat loss. In August or September usually gathers to feed in reed beds, where it can nearly double its weight before departing for Africa. Ringing studies have shown that Irish sedge warblers join British birds and migrate down the west coast of Europe to Africa. One sedge warbler, caught and ringed in County Cork, was retrapped in Cornwall the following morning!

Blackcap *Caipín Dubh*

W L=14

Sylvia atricapilla (PLATE 13)

MAIN FEATURES Male: cold brown-grey; pale throat and undertail; neat jet black cap. **Female**: slightly browner; less noticeable pale chestnut brown cap. Same size as a robin.

VOICE GUIDE The call is a harsh *tcek* repeated many times if alarmed. The song is a series of very varied warbling notes, becoming louder towards the end.

GENERAL INFORMATION Mainly a summer visitor from Africa to deciduous woodlands, where it can be difficult to see. Also overwinters in small numbers and is seen in gardens and at bird tables. Feeds on insects in summer and berries in the winter, when large areas of ivy are worth checking for this neat bird.

A scarce breeding warbler of open woodland. In recent years it has increased in numbers during the winter months, especially on the south and east coasts. It is most likely to be seen in gardens and visiting bird tables, where it behaves quite aggressively towards other birds.

Chiffchaff *Tiuf-teaf*

S L=11

Phylloscopus collybita (PLATE 11)

MAIN FEATURES A very small warbler. Upper parts green-grey; underside light yellow-grey; thin dark eye-stripe; narrow, pale, supercilium; legs and bill dark grey-black. **In flight**:

weak, slightly undulating flight; moves busily from branch to branch in search of insects on leaves; flicks wings and tail. This and the next species (willow warbler) are very difficult to distinguish except by their song.

VOICE GUIDE It gets its name from its song, which cannot be confused with any other species in Ireland. It is a loud strident bouncing *chiff-chaff-chiff-chiff-chaff* ... lasting five or more seconds at a time. The singing bird is often difficult to locate as it is hidden by foliage at the top of the tree canopy. Its call is a soft *wheeet*. Usually heard before the willow warbler, with overwintering birds singing as early as the beginning of March.

GENERAL INFORMATION A common summer visitor overall with slightly thinner distribution in the treeless areas of the west and at higher altitudes. Not found very far from deciduous trees.

Most winter south of the Sahara desert. It was quite scarce in Ireland in the last century, with the population increasing steadily in the first quarter of this century. During autumn migration chiffchaffs from Scandinavia and western Russia have been identified in Ireland.

CONFUSION SPECIES *Willow Warbler* (PLATE 11): see below.

Willow Warbler *Ceolaire Sailí* *

S L=11-12

Phylloscopus trochilus (PLATE 11)

MAIN FEATURES Similar in size, shape and pattern to the chiffchaff, but brighter and more yellow-looking; usually has pale legs.

VOICE GUIDE Its song is a loud clear cascading warble, quiet and slow at the start, louder and faster at the end, lasting three or four seconds. Call is a soft short *wooeet*, similar to chiffchaff.

GENERAL INFORMATION Far more common than the last species (chiffchaff) and indeed with at least 800,000 breeding pairs in Ireland the willow warbler

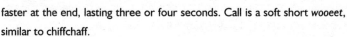

is our most common summer visitor. It arrives later than the chiffchaff, usually in April, and departs sooner. It occupies a wider range of habitats, and nests on or near the ground. During spring willow warblers from Scandinavia are occasionally seen in Ireland.

CONFUSION SPECIES *Chiffchaff* (PLATE 11): usually has dark legs; song completely different.

Goldcrest

Dreoilín Easpaig/ Dreolín Ceannbhuí

A   L=9

Regulus regulus (PLATE 12)

MAIN FEATURES Smallest bird in Europe. The centre of the crown is orange on the male, yellow on the female, bordered by black. **Adult**: a tiny bird, dark olive-green above and pale grey below. Wings are dark brown with pale edges to both primaries and secondaries forming a pale panel on the closed wing; noticeable buff wing bar; very short, thin black bill; pink-brown legs. Black eye looks relatively big, a feature accentuated by a broad pale area around the eye. **Immature**: young birds lack crown stripe. **In flight**: weak, slightly undulating flight, rapid wing beats. Flits from branch to branch and often hovers while catching insects on leaves.

VOICE GUIDE Its call, usually heard before the bird is seen, is a very thin, high-pitched, erratic *szitt-szitt-szitt*. Its song is again very high-pitched and includes a rapid *fh-he-hee*, usually repeated four times, followed by a similar more varied phrase.

GENERAL INFORMATION The goldcrest prefers conifers, especially spruce, but is also found in mixed woodland and even visits gardens. It is very common in Ireland, with over 500,000 breeding pairs. It feeds on insects which it catches by inspecting what appears to be every inch of every leaf it comes across. In summer it raises two broods, starting the second when the first is only half-grown, and laying eggs adding up to almost twice its body weight in one brood. In the winter, goldcrests from Britain and northern Europe join our own, and noticeable decreases in its population are recorded following severe winters.

Spotted Flycatcher *Cuilsealgaire*

S   L=14

Muscicapa striata (PLATE 11)

MAIN FEATURES The name is a bit misleading as there is streaking rather than spotting on adults. About the size of a robin, it is a plain-looking bird. The crown, which is peaked at the rear, is closely streaked grey-white and dark brown. Throat, breast and belly very pale grey-brown; dark streaks on breast and flanks; undertail coverts white; wings dark grey-brown, faint wing bar; back slightly paler. Usually seen alone, sitting erect on an exposed branch towards the bottom of a tree. **In flight**: darts out with a broad, agile sweep to catch an insect in mid-air, returning to the same position or to a nearby branch.

VOICE GUIDE Makes a low harsh *tsee* call and an unremarkable song.

GENERAL INFORMATION A summer visitor to our wooded areas. It gets its name from its characteristic behaviour of catching insects. One of the last of our summer visitors to arrive, usually in the first week of May, and very susceptible to cold wet weather during the breeding season. It has declined in recent years and weather conditions, both here and on its way south to its wintering grounds in southern Africa, are thought to be a major factor. Not as common in the west, away from deciduous trees or at higher altitudes.

Long-tailed Tit *Meantán Earrfhada*

W   L=12-14

Aegithalos caudatus (PLATE 13)

MAIN FEATURES Out-sized black and white tail, as long as its small pink, black and white body. *Upper parts*: head grey-white with broad black stripe above the eye; back and wings black with pink patches at the base of the wings; pale edges to the secondaries. *Underside*: throat and breast dirty white, becoming grey-pink on the belly and undertail; black eyes and legs; tiny bill. **In flight**: reluctant to fly even short distances. Weak, slightly undulating flight. Usually seen in flocks ranging in size from three or four to over twenty.

VOICE GUIDE Flocks in winter can be quite noisy, making a variety of calls, including a short low *chrup* and a faster thin *ssee-ssee-ssee*. Its song is similar to its call notes.

GENERAL INFORMATION It feeds mainly on small insects, though it will visit bird tables in winter and take peanuts. During winter nights the flock, which is comprised of family members and relatives, will huddle close together for warmth. Feeding in a flock helps them to find food more successfully and so survive the winter. In spring the flock breaks up and each pair sets up territory and starts building its very elaborate nest, containing sometimes up to 2,000 feathers, held together by spiders' webs, and made invisible by a covering of lichens. The nest is spherical and difficult to see. More common in east and southern half of the country.

Coal Tit *Meantán Dubh*

W L=11-12

Parus ater (PLATE 13)

MAIN FEATURES Long white patch on the nape; black head and white ear coverts. *Upper parts:* dark grey-brown, two faint white wing bars. *Underside:* pale buff-grey; bill short and thin; legs long and dark grey. Comes readily to bird tables and has a mischievous jizz. Dull in colour compared to the other tits. **In flight:** weak, bouncing flight, short bursts of rapid wing beats.

VOICE GUIDE Its calls and song are varied but include a high, forced *fee-chew* repeated several times. Also a very high, goldcrest-like *su-ee-ou, zit-zit-zit, su-ee-ou.*

GENERAL INFORMATION The coal tit is fond of wooded areas, with a particular preference for conifers and also sessile oak and birch. It is widespread in Ireland, absent only from treeless areas, particularly in the extreme west. Resident, rarely travelling far from its place of birth. In winter, it often forms part of a flock consisting of different members of the tit family. Unlike other members of the tit family, however, it hoards food at any time of the year and so does not suffer so much in severe weather. One person put out 250 grammes of whole peanuts on a bird table only to find that a coal tit had removed the lot in less than an hour, hiding the nuts in cracks in a nearby wall.

Blue Tit *Meantán Gorm* *

A L=11-12

Parus caeruleus (PLATE 13)

MAIN FEATURES A very colourful little bird. *Upper parts:* pale blue cap surrounded by a white halo; white ear coverts; dark line through the eye; back green-blue; wings blue with faint white wing bar; tail also blue. *Underside*: throat, side of the neck and nape dark blue; breast and belly pale yellow. **Immature**: similar in pattern to adults but more yellow in overall colour. **In flight**: weak, bouncing flight, rapid wing beats.

VOICE GUIDE Like most members of the tit family, the blue tit is very vocal and has various call notes. The most characteristic are a very high *pfit-pfit-che-ha-ah-ah* and a lower, scolding *churr*.

GENERAL INFORMATION One of our most common species with over one million pairs breeding. It has a wide habitat preference and is common everywhere in winter and absent only from exposed areas, particularly on the west coast, in the breeding season. Like the last species, the blue tit rarely travels far. Ringing studies have shown that in the course of a winter's day, what you thought were three or four birds visiting your bird-feeder may actually have been up to two hundred individuals, and over an average winter period you might unwittingly have played host to about a thousand different blue tits! Like all members of this family, the blue tit is very acrobatic and because it likes nesting in cracks in walls and trees it will usually take up residence in a nest-box in no time at all.

Great Tit *Meantán Mór* *

A L=14

Parus major (PLATE 13)

MAIN FEATURES The largest of this family and also very colourful. The head is jet black with bright white cheeks (ear coverts). *Upper parts*: dark blue-green; primaries, secondaries and tail feathers dark with varying degrees of pale blue edging; white wing bar; outer tail feather white (most noticeable from below). *Underside*: breast and belly bright yellow with a black line down the centre. The black line is broad on males and narrow and incomplete on females. White under tail coverts. **Immature**: like blue tits young birds are faded and more yellow-looking.

VOICE GUIDE When it comes to calls it is hard to beat the repertoire of the great tit. Calls and song include a blue tit-like *tchurrr* and distinct phrases usually repeated two to four times, one sounding like *teacher, teacher*! More mechanical and repetitive than blue tit or coal tit.

GENERAL INFORMATION As widespread as the blue tit though not so numerous, and not as common in the west. Again, like other members of the tit family, the great tit is mostly sedentary, though there is evidence of Continental birds arriving here in autumn. Because it is bigger and less acrobatic than its relatives, it spends more time looking for food on the ground. All members of the tit family are mainly insect-eaters in the breeding season and seed- and fruit-eaters at other times. Likes beech-mast and if there is a good crop will remain in woods later into autumn and winter. In bad beechmast years, it moves out of the woods in search of food sooner and turns up at bird tables earlier, where it is the dominant tit species.

Magpie *Snag Breac* *

A   L=44-48
Pica pica (PLATE 14)

MAIN FEATURES Black and white. *Upper parts*: blue-green sheen on the black feathers; black, wedge-ended tail as long as its body. *Underside*: belly and flanks white; breast, throat and head completely black; legs and bill black. **In flight**: long tail; black-and-white primaries; white 'braces' on the back.

VOICE GUIDE Call is a harsh mechanical *chakk-kackk-kackk* ... Song is more musical with high squeaks. Noisy when alarmed, e.g. nearby cat or bird of prey.

GENERAL INFORMATION It might be hard to believe but up to the end of the 17th century magpies were unheard of in Ireland. Since then they have spread to every corner of the island, but are most numerous in the east. In autumn large flocks can be seen, sometimes over a hundred together. Its ability to eat a wide variety of food, from insects and fruit to carrion, has made it very successful. One of the biggest myths in birdlife is that magpies are decimating our small-bird population. It is true that they will eat eggs and young of other birds, but many exhaustive studies have revealed that these food items comprise a very small part of their diet. Just because the magpie might not look as cute as the local cat does not justify its villainous reputation. Large numbers are shot each year. For example, between 1982 and 1984 in County Cork, the Federation of Cork County Gun Clubs reported that 12,905 were shot.

Jackdaw *Cág* *

A L=33

Corvus monedula (PLATE 14)

MAIN FEATURES Silver-grey nape and side of neck; rest of the head black; body a duller silver-grey; wings and tail black; pale blue eyes; bill fairly short, black and straight; legs black. A very neat-looking crow. **In flight**: short primary 'fingers'; flocks glide, twist and turn.

VOICE GUIDE Voice higher pitched than rook. Includes harsh *keyaak* and *kew-kaw* sometimes repeated several times.

GENERAL INFORMATION One of our most common crows, this bird is more common in towns and cities than the next species, the rook. It is probably best-known to most for its infamous habit of nesting in chimney pots. A common species and numerous everywhere, except parts of the extreme west. During the winter it will move away from exposed areas such as uplands.

This bird is closely associated with humans, and because of its agility is more numerous around refuse tips than the rook. During the breeding season, apart from nesting on buildings, it will also nest in hollow trees and on sea cliffs. The jackdaw scavenges in rubbish in towns and cities but also eat insects, snails and spiders. Often feeds in pasture land in the company of its near relative the rook. Often seen sitting in pairs on roofs in winter. It frequently roosts in large numbers, usually at traditional woodland sites, in company with other crow species.

CONFUSION SPECIES *Rook, especially young birds* (PLATE 14): see below.

Rook (Crow) *Préachán/Rúcach* *

A L=33
Corvus frugilegus (PLATE 14)

MAIN FEATURES All feathers black with a purple-blue sheen, duller when worn. Bill long and looks slightly down-curved. **Adult**: outer half of bill dark; inner half and bare throat patch powdery white; black legs and untidy feathers around the thighs, giving it a 'shaggy trousers' appearance. Not as neat-looking as the jackdaw, moves more slowly and deliberately on the ground, often 'galloping' away if approached. **Immature**: rooks in their first year have an all-black bill with black feathers on the inner half of the upper mandible. **In flight**: the primaries can clearly be seen as 'fingers' at the end of the wings, not so noticeable on jackdaws.

VOICE GUIDE Call is a typical *kaw*, uttered on its own or repeated several times; often fans its tail and stretches forward when calling.

GENERAL INFORMATION One of the first comments of visiting birdwatchers from abroad concerns the abundance of crows on this island. The rook is by far the most common crow species we have, absent only from treeless areas in the extreme west. Unlike the jackdaw, it prefers rural areas, especially where there is a good mixture of pasture and arable crops. It nests in colonies called rookeries, liking Scots pines, but any tall trees will do. Rookeries can vary from a few scattered pairs, to many hundreds of nests tightly packed together. The sound of a rookery in spring and summer is as much part of the countryside as cows and sheep. The rook is omnivorous, that is it has a varied diet. In winter it follows very specific flight paths to roost sites that may contain thousands of individuals. In late summer and autumn on these flight paths a large procession of crows can be seen going to roost for the night.

CONFUSION SPECIES *Raven* (PLATE 14): much bigger; massive black bill; wedge-shaped tail. *Jackdaw* (PLATE 14): smaller; silver-grey on head; pale eyes. *Chough* (PLATE 14): mainly seen on headlands; red down-curved bill and long red legs; glossy black plumage (name pronounced 'chuff').

Hooded Crow (Grey or Scald Crow) *Feannóg* *

A   L=47

Corvus corone (PLATE 14)

MAIN FEATURES Black hood covering head, neck and breast (forms a rough-edged bib); rest of the body pale grey-brown; wings and tail black; bill strong and black, legs dark. The same size as a rook. **In flight**: obvious, pale, grey-brown back. When moulting, wings can sometimes look striped black and white.

VOICE GUIDE Its call is usually a loud hoarse *krraaa-krraaa-krraaa*.

GENERAL INFORMATION This is the most widespread of the crow family though not as abundant as the rook. Always nests alone, usually in trees, but where none are available will use cliff ledges, shrubs and even the ground itself. It has a wide taste in food, including insects, amphibians, small birds, grain and carrion, which partly explains why it is so widespread. It is the only crow that regularly gathers food on the seashore, where it can often be seen flying up from the shore and dropping shellfish onto the rocks or the road to break them open, often resulting in large numbers of broken shells left mysteriously on top of walls and on coastal roads. In Britain, the hooded crow is confined to Scotland and the Isle of Man, and is replaced elsewhere by the carrion crow, which is the same species but has all-black plumage.

Raven *Fiach Dubh*

A   L=65
Corvus corax (PLATE 14)

MAIN FEATURES Largest Irish crow. One and a half times the size of the rook and twice the size of the jackdaw. All black plumage; massive bill, feathers extending out the upper mandible. **In flight**: shows very obvious primary 'fingers'. Tail wedge-ended, not round- or square-ended like the rook or jackdaw.

VOICE GUIDE The call is also characteristic, given either in flight or from a perch, when it often bobs its head up and down. It is a deep *ooooaawk* usually repeated several times.

GENERAL INFORMATION While not a very common bird, the raven is not easily forgotten once seen. Once common over most of Ireland, by the end of the 19th century, as a result of persecution by farmers and hunting interests, this magnificent bird was to be found only in remote uplands and offshore islands. Since the beginning of this century, pressure has eased and it continues to expand its range back into lowland areas. Usually nests on rock ledges, in large trees and on ruined buildings. While carrion forms a major part of its diet it will readily take small live mammals, frogs, lizards and insects.

Non-breeding flocks can sometimes contain over 50 birds, and from the tops of some of our highest mountains, you can often see them as dots above your head, calling or performing their characteristic tumbling flights, usually during courtship.

CONFUSION SPECIES *Rook* (PLATE 14): young birds smaller; shorter tail is square- or round-ended.

Starling *Druid* *

A L=21
Sturnus vulgaris (PLATE 7)

MAIN FEATURES Slightly smaller than a blackbird. **Adult in winter**: dark glossy plumage; heavily spotted, most concentrated on the head which can look pale at a distance. These spots become less obvious as spring approaches. Bill dark, pointed, dull pink. **Adult in summer**: black plumage with blue and green sheen; few spots, restricted to back and towards tail; bill straw yellow, very pale blue-grey base; legs pink. **Immature**: dusty grey-brown; pale throat, pale buff edges to wing feathers; bill black; legs dark brown-red. Rarely seen alone, always quarrelling and noisy. **In flight**: all dark; triangular shaped wings; short, fanned tail.

VOICE GUIDE The calls and songs of the starling are very varied and it is an expert mimic, not only of other birds but also of referees' whistles, door bells and even car alarms, all mixed up together.

GENERAL INFORMATION Common and widespread, absent only from some upland areas. During the breeding season requires a crevice to make its nest in and grassland nearby for gathering food. These requirements are amply provided by man in the form of the walls and eaves of houses, farmland in rural areas and lawns and parkland in urban and suburban areas. It catches insects by sticking its long thin bill into the grass and opening it wide causing any insects to fall into the space, which can then be easily caught if suitable.

In the late autumn and winter, starlings form into large flocks, often landing on pylons and overhead wires, before going to roost in woods and reedbeds or on cliffs and buildings. These flocks often contain many thousands of birds, sometimes as many as 100,000. Each winter Irish starlings are joined by birds from Britain, Scandinavia, Germany and Poland. In severe Continental winters many more come and as many as six to eight million may stay here.

CONFUSION SPECIES *Blackbird* (PLATE 10): bigger, no spots, long tail.

House Sparrow *Gealbhán Binne* *

A L=15

Passer domesticus (PLATE 15)

MAIN FEATURES Male: black bib, smaller in the winter; grey crown; dark brown eye-stripe extends and widens back and down the nape. Ear coverts and side of throat pale grey, sometimes looking almost white. Breast and belly pencil-grey; tail fairly long, dark-brown with paler buff edges to the feathers; rump grey; back streaked light and dark brown; wings light and dark brown; white wing bar. **Female**: no distinctive plumage features, paler, lacking the black, white and richer browns of the male. **In flight**: fast and straight, undulates on longer flights.

VOICE GUIDE The call is a loud *cheep*, repeated without variation. Often heard calling and chattering in groups from bushes or hedges, where their dull colours make them almost invisible, despite the loud noise.

GENERAL INFORMATION With an estimated world population of five hundred million, the house sparrow is considered to be one of the most widespread and numerous land-bird species in the world. This is reflected in Ireland where up to 1.4 million pairs bred during 1988-91. It is encountered everywhere and is most numerous in the eastern half of the island. As the name suggests it has been associated with man for a long time. It nests in holes in buildings and walls, and will use house martin and sand martin nests, or build nests in bushes. In winter it will eat a large variety of foods and large flocks can often be heard noisily chattering from the depths of an evergreen hedge or bush. Can often be seen 'dust-bathing' in dust or sand, usually in small groups. This is thought to help remove parasites and keep plumage in good condition. It is a sedentary species and has declined in some areas in recent years. Changes in farming practices, crop-spraying and the use of pesticides in gardens are contributing factors. One study showed that cats accounted for 30 percent of house sparrow deaths in a village in England.

CONFUSION SPECIES *Tree Sparrow* (PLATE 15): found in a few areas; differs in head pattern with crown completely chestnut brown; cheeks white with isolated black spot; sexes similar.

Chaffinch *Rí Rua* *

A   L=15-16
Fringilla coelebs (PLATE 15)

MAIN FEATURES Male: face, breast and belly rosy orange-pink; undertail white; crown and nape metallic blue-grey; back brown; rump olive-green. Wings dark brown with two white wing bars; white outer tail feathers on a relatively long dark tail. Males in their first year are duller, though not as dull as the females. **Female**: same pattern as male but drab pale grey-brown. **In flight**: double white wing bars and white outer tail feathers very obvious. White underwing.

VOICE GUIDE Calls include a loud *buzz-twink-twink-twink* and in flight a low, weak *weiou*. Its song, which lasts about three seconds and is repeated, starts with buzzing notes, slows and descends into a jumble and finally a flourish.

GENERAL INFORMATION Possibly the most abundant and widespread breeding species in Ireland with an estimated 2,100,000 breeding pairs during 1988-91. It nests in woodlands, hedges and bushes, anywhere in the country. It feeds its young on many types of insect caught on foliage or on the ground. Irish chaffinches are sedentary, with most breeding pairs returning to the same nest site year after year. In the winter, millions of chaffinches arrive here from northern Europe, via European countries bordering the south shore of the North Sea. Irish birds feed more in woodland areas and gardens, while the visiting birds, which are larger and paler, prefer to feed in large flocks in open fields. Common everywhere but far more numerous in the eastern half of the country. Outside the breeding season, chaffinches mainly eat seeds, and over a hundred different seed types have been recorded for this species, which is one possible explanation for why it is so abundant.

CONFUSION SPECIES *Brambling* (NOT ILLUSTRATED): uncommon winter visitor; white rump; male more orange then red; less white on wings. *Greenfinch* (PLATE 15): absence of white on females and immatures (see below).

Greenfinch *Glasán Darach*

A L=15
Carduelis chloris (PLATE 15)

MAIN FEATURES Male: bright yellow-green; bright yellow patches on the wings and base of the outer tail feathers; grey on wings and ear coverts; Strong, conical bill often pink at the base; pink legs. **Female**: drab, paler yellow patches. Male and female both have a dark shadow around the eye. **Immature**: streaked below and may resemble female chaffinches (see above). **In flight**: flashes yellow and green. Undulating flight.

VOICE GUIDE Calls include a squeaky *whou-ie-ouh*, and buzzing notes. Will sometimes sing during a display flight, with stiff mechanical wing beats. Parts of its long, melodious, twittering song are often likened to that of a canary.

GENERAL INFORMATION This species frequents arable farm land and suburban areas, so it is not surprising that it is more common in the east and south. It nests in trees and bushes, usually in fairly open habitat, and suburban areas have become important for breeding. The young are fed mainly on seeds but some insects are also given. The increased use of herbicides on farmland has contributed to its decline in recent years. In winter only a few birds come to Ireland, mainly from Britain. As winter progresses and the supply of seed diminishes, they form large flocks, sometimes containing over a hundred birds. They are regular visitors to bird tables and fight fiercely between themselves and with other species for the best place on the peanut-feeder. Threatening with its bill open and wings spread, it will tangle upwards into the air with a rival with a flurry of wings before separating.

CONFUSION SPECIES *Siskin* (PLATE 15): smaller. Male: black cap and chin; female and immature: very streaked; black and yellow wings.

Goldfinch *Lasair Choille*

A   L=14
Carduelis carduelis (PLATE 16)

MAIN FEATURES Blood-red, white and black head. *Upper parts*: broad bright yellow wing bars; rest of wings black, with white tips to the primaries and secondaries; tail black and white; back is pale golden brown; rump is paler again. *Underside*: white with broad golden-brown flanks; incomplete sandy-brown breast band. Birds just out of the nest are similar to the adults except that the head is completely pale brown. **In flight**: striking yellow and black wing pattern. Undulating flight. Rarely seen alone. Does not usually flock with other finch species.

VOICE GUIDE It has a long beautiful song, containing buzzes, characteristic fluid notes, trills and twitters. Calls almost continuously in flight. The call is simpler than the song and contains more fluid notes.

GENERAL INFORMATION A bird which declined in numbers in the last century due to large-scale trapping, especially in the northern half of the island. The introduction of laws protecting birds in this century has reduced this activity but illegal trapping still continues in some parts. In Ireland it is sedentary by nature, usually nesting in trees but occasionally in bushes. Like many of its relatives it nests in loose colonies. It is not easy to see as it is constantly on the move, searching for its main food – thistles – for which its long thin bill is specially adapted. It will also feed on the seeds of knapweed, ragworts, groundsel and dandelions. It is the only finch that can extract the seeds from the teasel (a plant used widely for flower-arranging). In the last twenty years it has declined in many areas which may be due to the increased use of herbicides.

Siskin *Píobaire*

W   L=12

Carduelis spinus (PLATE 15)

MAIN FEATURES Smaller than a robin. **Male:** black cap and throat; head dark olive-green with pale yellow stripe extending from the eye back to the nape and down around the ear coverts; wings black with two bright yellow wing bars and pale edges to the secondaries; back olive-green with faint dark streaks; rump yellow, short notched tail with yellow patches at base of outer feathers; breast and upper belly green-yellow; lower belly and undertail coverts white with dark streaking. **Female**: no black cap or chin; not as yellow, especially on the wings; heavier streaking on the back. **Immature**: paler and more streaked than female. **In flight**: yellow and black; fast and undulating. Visits bird-feeders in late winter.

VOICE GUIDE Calls and song include a variable twitter, a very thin *tee-oou*, a buzzing *wheeeze* and a high, bouncing, chattering trill.

GENERAL INFORMATION A finch that breeds mainly in coniferous plantations, particularly spruce. The recent increase in afforestation has led to a corresponding increase in its population. In winter it is has become a regular visitor to bird tables where it can be very aggressive. It has a characteristic habit of perching upside down when feeding from peanut feeders, particularly those that are red. Numbers visiting gardens vary from year to year, depending on the availability of natural food supplies. Often seen feeding with redpolls in alder woods in winter.

Linnet *Gleoiseach*

A L=14

Carduelis cannabina (PLATE 16)

MAIN FEATURES Male: in summer, bright red forehead and breast patches; rest of the head grey; white belly; back rich brown; wings darker brown, bright white edges to the primaries; tail notched and edged white. Duller in winter, losing its bright red feathers. **Female** and **immature**: browner, streaked, no red or grey. **In flight**: diffuse white flashes on wings, calls constantly, bouncing flight.

VOICE GUIDE Its flight call is squeaky, like a wet cork rubbed against glass. Its song is often a very long series of chirps, twitters, chatters and musical, warbling notes. Often sings from the top of a bush or tree.

GENERAL INFORMATION This finch is associated with cultivated lands though can be found anywhere weed seeds are available, from high ground to seashore and islands. It likes to nest in dense cover, and is often found in areas of gorse during the breeding season. It is surprisingly scarce in southwest Ulster. During the winter many of our linnets migrate to France and Spain, and those that remain rarely travel far, but form flocks of up to 200 birds. It does usually mix with other finch species and when disturbed will fly around in a circle before returning to the ground. Sadly, like many wild birds associated with farming, the linnet has declined noticeably in the last twenty years and intensification of farming, with the associated increasein the use of herbicides and hedge-removal, may be to blame.

CONFUSION SPECIES *Redpoll* (PLATE 15): smaller; black chin; almost no white on wings (see below).

Redpoll *Gleoisín Cúldearg*

W   L=12-13

Carduelis flammea (PLATE 15)

MAIN FEATURES Male: blood-red forehead; black bib; back streaked light and dark brown; wings darker with two pale buff wing bars, the inner one being very faint; rump pale with faint dark streaks; tail short and slightly notched; breast deep pink in breeding season, buff in winter; belly and undertail coverts white; flanks heavily streaked light and dark brown; short, stubby, pale yellow bill; legs short and black. **Female** and **immature**: duller and more streaked. **In flight**: very bouncy flight.

VOICE GUIDE Calls and song include a high, thin rising *oiu-eeee*, also short, fast reeling notes and a *chi-chi-chi-chaa*.

GENERAL INFORMATION A woodland finch which breeds mainly in the north-west half of the country. Birch and alder seeds form the main part of its diet. It has declined as a breeding species in recent years, especially in the south-eastern half of the country. In winter it is never found far from alders and birch, feeding acrobatically, often in the company of siskins. Redpolls of the north European and Greenland races have been seen in Ireland.

CONFUSION SPECIES *Linnet* (PLATE 16): bigger; less streaked; obvious white on wing.

Bullfinch *Corcán Coille*

A L=16

Pyrrhula pyrrhula (PLATE 16)

MAIN FEATURES A large, fat finch. **Male**: jet-black crown and nape; throat, breast and belly vivid, deep pink; light grey back; black wings with a broad white wing bar; large white rump patch (best seen in flight); black tail; undertail coverts white; bill short and heavy. **Female**: vivid pink replaced by dull pale grey-brown; back also grey-brown; grey nape. **Immature**: like female but lacks black cap. **In flight**: bouncing flight, always showing bright white rump.

VOICE GUIDE Song is a soft whistling chatter, the call a weak, soft *weeep*.

GENERAL INFORMATION This finch is very common in Ireland, being absent only from the extreme west and high altitudes. Despite this and the colourful plumage of the male it is not seen very often. In fact the large white rump patch is often the first indication of its presence. It nests in thick undergrowth and the birds feed on insects when rearing young. For the rest of the year seeds are their main food. Between February and April if natural food supplies are low it will take to eating buds from fruit trees. Research has shown that a fruit tree can lose up to 50 percent of its buds in spring without affecting the crop. The main problem is that it usually feeds only in trees at the edge of an orchard and these can suffer badly in some years. A sedentary species, usually seen alone or in pairs. Recent farming trends such as intensification and hedge removal have contributed to their decline in some areas.

Yellowhammer *Buíóg* *

A   L=16-17
Emberiza citrinella (PLATE 16)

MAIN FEATURES Summer: male has bright yellow head, female duller; back, wings and tail a complex mixture of light and dark browns; rump bright red-brown; yellow throat and breast, streaked on female; chestnut side of breast and streaked flanks on male. **Winter**: dull-looking; males and females similar in appearance, heavy grey-brown streaking on head, throat, breast and flanks, with yellow tinges to the head, throat, and lower belly. **In flight**: looks long and slim. White outer tail feathers; rusty rump.

VOICE GUIDE Like some other birds, the yellowhammer is often first located by its distinctive song in spring and summer. It is a loud clear wheezing song, with the notes spaced as if saying rather quickly *little-bit-of-bread-and no cheeeeese*. Its call is a short rough *schep*.

GENERAL INFORMATION This bird feeds mainly on the seeds of large grasses and cereals. It normally nests on the ground in tall grasses near hedges, walls or bushes. It is usually seen on its own in the breeding season, on the ground or singing from a wall or the top of a bush in open farmland. In winter it sometimes forms flocks containing up to 100 birds. Does not travel far from its place of birth and is most numerous in the east and south, and across the midlands. It has declined dramatically in the last twenty years, particularly in the west and north. Areas where tillage comprises less than 10 percent of land use have seen large declines. Also the switch from spring to autumn sowing of cereals has meant less food in winter.

CONFUSION SPECIES *Reed Bunting*, female (PLATE 16): see below.

Reed Bunting *Gealóg Dhucheannac*

A L=15-16

Emberiza schoeniclus (PLATE 16)

MAIN FEATURES Male: very striking in summer plumage. Black head, white neck collar and moustache; back heavily streaked dark brown and buff; rump grey; wings have rich brown tones, no white; tail long and black with white outer feathers; underside pale grey; black streaks on the flanks. **Female** and **immature**: less striking; dark brown heads, white throat and moustache; faint white supercilium; no white neck collar. In winter males resemble females, and the plumage is paler. **In flight**: undulating, rarely flies far; chestnut on wings; white outer tail feathers.

VOICE GUIDE Call is a high, thin, descending *tzeeeu*. Its song, usually sung from a prominent position, is a high, hesitant, buzzing variation on *weeet-weet-chit* and a lower, faster *chi-choo*.

GENERAL INFORMATION A common breeding species throughout the island, though not so abundant in the south. Usually nests on the ground not far from water, in reedbeds, bogs and along ditches, also in young conifer plantations. During the breeding season it feeds on insects, changing to seeds of small grasses and herbs in winter, when it roams in small flocks over open ground in search of food. The reed bunting has declined in numbers in recent times, due mainly to modern farming practices and habitat loss.

CONFUSION SPECIES *Yellowhammer* (PLATE 16): superficially females and immatures may look similar; yellower; no white moustachial stripe; rusty rump.

Birdwatching in Ireland

While you have a good chance of seeing birds anywhere in Ireland, there are places which, for a variety of reasons, attract more species. Some places have become very famous for birds, such as Lough Neagh, the North Bull, the Wexford Slobs and the Skellig Rocks. Ireland has such a low human population that there are many areas of the country that have never been studied in detail for birds. The following is a county-by-county list of sites noted for birdwatching in Ireland. It is by no means exhaustive and if you need advice on places to go, contact the IWC in the Republic or the RSPB in Northern Ireland, who will give you all the information you need. Not all sites listed have unchecked access, so please enquire locally before entering what might be private property.

For more detailed information with maps, on these and other sites, Clive Hutchinson's *Where To Watch Birds In Ireland* (Gill and Macmillan, 1994) is a must.

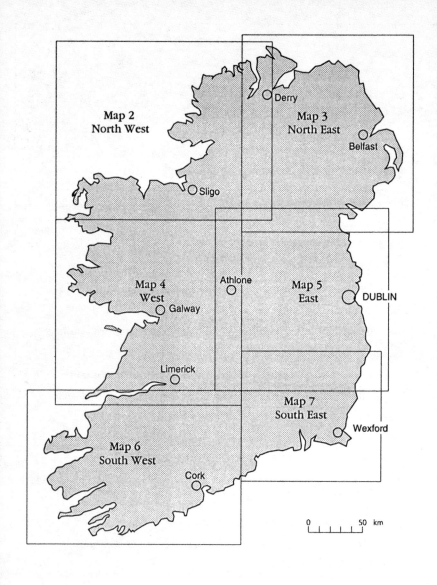

MAP I – Ireland

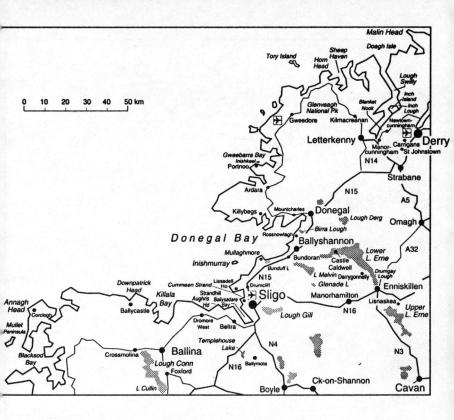

MAP 2 – North West

MAP 3 – North East

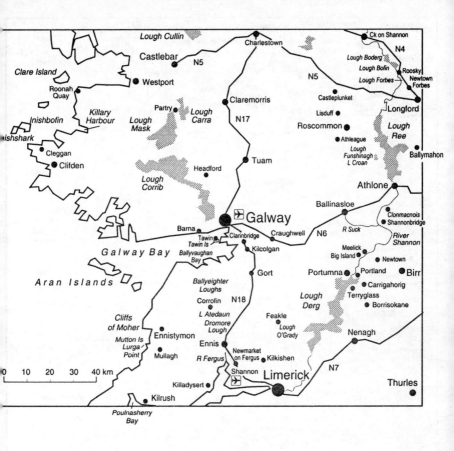

MAP 4 – West

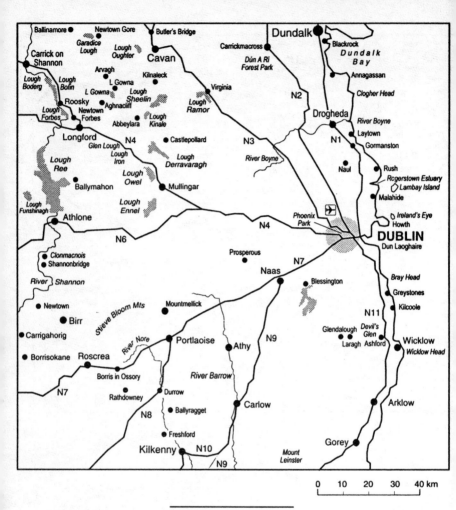

MAP 5 – East

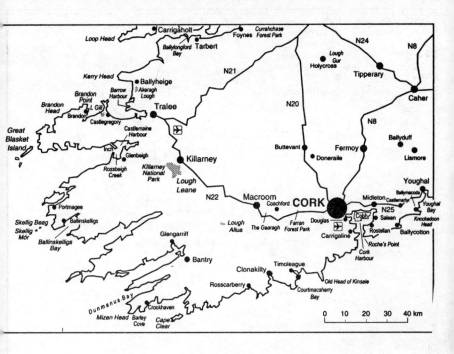

MAP 6 – South West

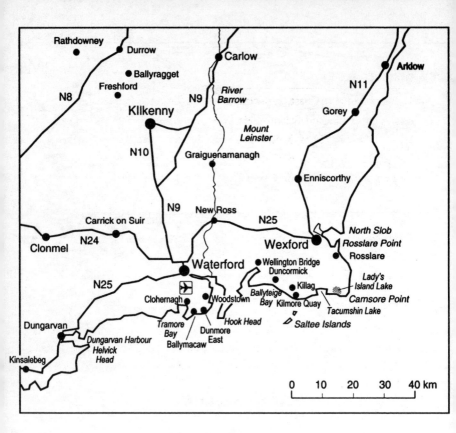

MAP 7 – South East

Antrim (map 3)

1. North Antrim Coast, especially the long-distance footpath between Bushmills and Ballintoy Harbour. 2. Murlough Bay and Fair Head near Ballycastle. 3. Rathlin Island. 4. Larne Lough. 5. Belfast Lough (North shore). 6. Carrickfergus. 7. Loughshore Park, near Jordanstown. 8. Duncrue Street Marsh, three kilometres north of Belfast, near Duncrue Road. 9. Lough Neagh. 10. Shane's Castle, an RSPB reserve on the north shore of Lough Neagh. 11. Rea's Wood, three kilometres south of Shane's Castle, behind the Deer Park Hotel. 12. Garry Bog, eight kilometres north of Ballymoney. 13. Lough Beg, north of Lough Neagh, just north of Toome.

Armagh (map 3)

1. South shore of Lough Neagh. 2. Oxford Island Nature Reserve, north of Lurgan. 3. Craigavon Balancing Lakes. 4. Lurgan Park Lake. 5. Annaghroe, beside the Blackwater river, two kilometres southwest of Caledon.

Carlow (map 5)

1. Oak Park, near Carlow Town. 2. Barrow River. 3. Mount Leinster.

Cavan (map 5)

1. Lough Oughter, south-west of Butler's Bridge. 2. Lough Gowna, south-east of Arvagh. 3. Lough Ramor, in Virginia. 4. The shores of Lough Sheelin, south of Kilnaleck.

Clare (map 4 and 6)

1. Shannon Estuary near Shannon Town. 2. Fergus estuary, on the eastern side at Ing (best vantage point) west of Newmarket-on-Fergus, and at Islandavanna east of Teermaclane. 3. Clonderalaw Bay, between Labasheeda and Killadysert. 4. Poulnasherry Bay, between

Kilrush and Querrin. 5. Bridges of Ross, near Loop Head. 6. Loop Head. 7. Lough Donnell, south of Mullach. 8. Lurga Point, east of Mutton Island. 9. Mutton Island. 10. Cliffs of Moher, west of Ennistimon. 11. Ballyvaughan Bay. 12. Ballyeighter Loughs, Lough Cullaun, Ballycullinan Lough, and especially Lough Atedaun near Corrofin. 13. Dromore Lough. 14. Lough O'Grady, south-east of Feakle. 15. Lough Cullaunyheeda, north of Kilkishen. 16. Ballyallia Lake, just north of Ennis.

Cork (map 6)

1. Youghal Bay. 2. Foxhole, on the right-hand side of the main Youghal-Dungarvan road about two kilometres north of Youghal. 3. Ballymacoda Bay. 4. Knockadoon Head and Capel Island (no access to the Island). 5. Ballycotton and Ballynamona Strand. 6. Roche's Point, at the mouth of Cork Harbour. 7. Cork Harbour, sites include: Rostellan; Saleen Creek, one kilometre west of Saleen village; Cobh and Great Island; Douglas estuary; Lough Beg, an IWC Reserve, east of Carrigaline. 8. Old Head of Kinsale; Kinsale Marsh, two kilometres west of Kinsale. 9. Courtmacsherry Bay, from Kilbrittain, through Timoleague as far as Courtmacsherry. 10. Clonakilty Bay. 11. Rosscarbery Estuary. 12. Cape Clear Island. 13. Mizen Head. 14. Lissagriffin, near Barleycove. 15. Crookhaven. 16. Dunmanus Bay. 17. Glengarriff Wood, on the main Glengarriff-Killarney road. 18. Lough Allua and the Gearagh, three kilometres west of Macroom, on the Cork-Killarney road. 19. Farran Wood, between Ovens and Coachford. 20. Kilcolman Wildfowl Refuge, near Buttevant/Doneraile. This is a National Nature Reserve, and access is strictly by permission only: contact Mrs M. Ridgway (Telephone: 022-24200). 21. Loughaderry, on the main Midleton-Castlemartyr road. 22. The Lough, Cork City.

Derry (map 3)

1. Lough Foyle, between Derry and Magilligan including Donny-brewer, Eglinton Station, Longfield, Roe estuary and Magilligan Point.
2. Gortmore, near Downhill, midway between Magilligan and Coleraine. 3. Bann estuary, left off the A2 at Articlave. 4. Portstewart Point, east of Portstewart Harbour. 5. Ramore Head, near Portrush.
6. Portrush, at the Countryside Centre and Skerries Islands. 7. Lough Beg, just north of Toome, on the Antrim border.

Donegal (map 2)

1. Donegal Bay. 2. Rossnowlagh and Birra Lough, between Donegal Town and Ballyshannon. 3. Mountcharles, west of Donegal Town. 4. Killybegs. 5. Sheskinmore Lough, north of Ardara. 6. Gweebarra Bay, especially between Portnoo and Inishkeel. 7. Horn Head. 8. Tory Island. 9. Sheep Haven, west of Dunfanaghy. 10. Lough Swilly, especially Inch Lough, on the main road to Inch Island. 11. Blanket Nook, north of Newtown Cunningham (also Rathmelton). 12. Big Isle, near Manorcunningham. 13. Malin Head, and nearby Inishtrahull. 14. Trawbreaga Bay and Isle of Doagh, west of Malin Village. 15. Carrigans to Saint Johnstown, south-west of Derry city. 16. Glenveagh National Park, midway between Kilmacrenan and Gweedore.

Down (map 3)

1. Kinnegar, five kilometres north-east of Belfast, near Hollywood.
2. Seashore footpath from Hollywood to Bangor. 3. Groomsport, three kilometres east of Bangor. 4. Copeland Island from Donaghadee. 5. Strangford Lough. 6. Castle Espie, three kilometres south-east of Comber. 7. Reagh Island, south towards Mahee Island from Castle Espie. 8. Whiterock, from Comber via Ardmillan. 9. Island Hill, four kilometres north-east of Comber, just off the road

to Newtownards. 10. The Maltings, two kilometres south of New-townards. 11. Greyabbey, eleven kilometres south-east of New-townards. 12. Castleward, near Strangford Village. 13. Dundrum Bay and Inner Dundrum Bay, contact the wardens at the Murlough National Nature Reserve (owned by the National Trust), on the west side of the bay south of Dundrum. 14. Carlingford Lough, north shore. 15. Clea Lakes, three kilometres from Killyleagh. 16. Quoile Pondage, north-east of Downpatrick. 17. Lagan Towpath, from Belfast to Lisburn. 18. Belvoir Park Forest, on the south side of Belfast, location of the Headquarters of the RSPB in Northern Ireland.

Dublin (map 5)

1. Rush. 2. Knock Lake, near Naul, off the main Dublin to Belfast Road. 3. Rogerstown estuary. 4. Malahide estuary. 5. Baldoyle estu-ary. 6. North Bull, south of Baldoyle on the north side of Dublin Bay. 7. Sandymount Strand, especially on or close to high tide. 8. Poolbeg Lighthouse, at the end of the South Wall. 9. Booterstown, just south of Merrion Gates. 10. West Pier, Dun Laoghaire. 11. Phoenix Park. 12. Dublin parks and canals.

Fermanagh (map 2)

1. Upper Lough Erne. 2. Lower Lough Erne, especially the RSPB reserve at the western end at Castle Caldwell. 3. Murlough Lake, near Lisnaskea. 4. Colebrook River, west of Lisnaskea. 5. Lough Navar Forest, off the main Enniskillen-Belleek road near Derrygon-nelly. 6. Drumgay Lough, five kilometres north of Enniskillen.

Galway (map 4)

1. Aran Islands. 2. Inishbofin and Inishshark off Cleggan, north-west of Clifden. 3. Galway Bay, including Tawin Island, west of Clarinbridge, Nimmo's Pier at the Claddagh in the heart of Galway

city, and Rusheen Bay, near Barna. 4. Lough Corrib. 5. Rostaff Lake, near Headford. 6. Rahasane Turlough, between Craughwell and Kilcolgan. 7. Coole, just north of Gort. 8. River Suck. 9. Portumna.

Kerry (map 6)

1. Ballinskelligs Bay. 2. Little Skellig and Great Skellig, by ferry from Portmagee and Ballinskelligs. 3. Rossbeigh Creek, at Glenbeigh to Inch, including Castlemaine Harbour. 4. Great Blasket. 5. Brandon Point, north of Brandon village. 6. Lough Gill, near Castlegregory. 7. Tralee Bay. 8. Barrow Harbour. 9. Akeragh Lough, south of Ballyheige. 10. Kerry Head, north of Ballyheige. 11. Ballylongford Bay. 12. Tarbert Bay. 13. Lough Leane. 14. Killarney National Park.

Kildare (map 5)

1. Prosperous reservoir.

Kilkenny (maps 5 and 7)

1. Tibberoughney Marsh, two kilometres south-east of Piltown. 2. Kilkenny City: Kilkenny Castle pond, Newtownpark Marsh behind the Newpark Hotel, Riverside drive on the south side. 3. Jenkinstown Wood, halfway between Kilkenny and Ballyragget. 4. The Barrow Walk at Graignamanagh.

Laois (map 5)

1. Slieve Bloom Mountains. 2. The 'Curragh', between Rathdowney and Durrow. 3. Lough Annaghmon, north-west of Mountmellick. 4. River Nore (near Borris-in-Ossory).

Leitrim (maps 3, 4 and 5)

1. Lough Allen. 2. Garadice Lough, between Ballinamore and Newtown Gore. 3. Lough Boderg and Lough Bofin, north-west of Roosky.

4. Glenade Lake, between Manorhamilton and Bundoran.

Limerick (map 6)

1. Shannon estuary between Foynes and Ringmoylan Quay. 2. Limerick City. 3. Lough Gur, south of Limerick City near Holycross. 4. Westfields, near Limerick City on the Shannon road. 5. Curragh Chase Forest Park, five kilometres south-east of Askeaton.

Longford (maps 4 and 5)

1. Inny River, and Barley Harbour near Ballymahon. 2. Lough Forbes and Castleforbes demesne, near Newtown Forbes. 3. Lough Kinale, near Abbeylara, Lough Gowna, near Aughnacliff.

Louth (maps 3 and 4)

1. Carlingford Lough, from Greenore to Omeath. 2. Dundalk Bay, including Ballymascanlan Bay, South Marsh, east of Dundalk at Soldier's Point, Lurgangreen, near Blackrock, and Annagassan. 3. Clogher Head. 4. Boyne estuary, east of Drogheda.

Mayo (maps 2 and 4)

1. Clare Island. 2. Killary Harbour to Roonagh Quay coastline. 3. Blacksod Bay. 4. Downpatrick Head, north of Ballycastle. 5. Mullet Peninsula. 6. Annagh Head. 7. Termoncarragh Lake near Corclogh. 8. Lough Conn and Lough Cullen, east of Foxford. 9. Lough Carra, east of Partry.

Meath (map 5)

1. Laytown. 2. Gormanston.

Monaghan (map 3)

1. Lough Egish, south of Castleblayney. 2. Dun a Rí Forest Park, south of Carrickmacross.

Offaly (map 4)

1. Little Brosna, from Newbridge, seven kilometres north-west of Birr, to Meelick. 2. Cloghan Castle. 3. Big Island and Friar's Island, north-west of Newtown. 4. Shannon River, at Clonmacnoise and Shannonbridge.

Roscommon (map 4)

1. River Shannon. 2. River Suck, between Ballyforan and Ballinasloe. 3. Lough Ree. 4. Cloonlaughnan, near Mount Talbot. 5. Briarfield, Castleplunket and Mullygollan Turlough, near Castleplunket. 6. Lisduff, north-west of Roscommon Town. 7. Lough Funshinagh and Lough Croan, south-east of Athleague.

Sligo (map 2)

1. Killala Bay. 2. Aughris Head, between Beltra and Dromore West. 3. Ballysadare Bay. 4. Cummeen Strand, east of Strandhill. 5. Drumcliff. 6. Lissadell. 7. Inishmurray. 8. Bunduff Lake, near Mullaghmore. 9. Lough Gill, especially the Hazelwood peninsula. 10. Templehouse Lake, north-west of Ballymote.

Tipperary (maps 4 and 5)

1. Little Brosna. 2. River Shannon. 3. Redfern Lough, between Borrisokane and Terryglass. 4. Slevoir Bay, in the north-east corner of Lough Derg between Carrigahorig and Portland. 5. Lough Avan.

Tyrone (map 3)

1. Western shore of Lough Neagh. 2. Sperrin Mountains.

Waterford (maps 6 and 7)

1. Woodstown. 2. Dunmore East. 3. Ballymacaw Glen, west of Dunmore East. 4. Brownstown Head, west of Ballymacaw. 5. Tra-

more Bay, especially Tramore Back Strand near the Rabbit Burrows just east of Tramore, also at Lissalan. 6. Dungarvan Harbour, especially from the Cunnigar sandspit. 7. Helvick Head. 8. Kinsalebeg, opposite Youghal. 9. Ballyshunnock reservoir, near Waterford City. 10. Coolfin, on the River Suir, midway between Waterford City and Carrig-on-Suir. 11. River Blackwater, especially between Lismore and Ballyduff.

Westmeath (map 5)

1. Lough Derravaragh, south-west of Castlepollard. 2. Lough Ennel, south-west of Mullingar. 3. Lough Owel, Lough Iron and Glen Lough north-west of Mullingar on the Dublin-Sligo road. 4. Lough Ree. 5. Shannon River.

Wexford (map 7)

1. North Slob, especially the Visitors' Centre on the OPW/IWC reserve which is signposted on the right, three kilometres north of Wexford town, on the Gorey road. 2. South Slob. 3. Rosslare back strand, through Rosslare village to Rosslare Point. 4. Carnsore Point. 5. Great Saltee, from Kilmore Quay. 6. Lady's Island Lake and Tacumshin Lake, between Carnsore Point and Kilmore Quay. 7. The Cull Bank on the western shore of Ballyteige Bay at Killag and Duncormick. 8. Bannow Bay, near Wellingtonbridge. 9. Hook Head.

Wicklow (map 5)

1. Bray Head. 2. Greystones to Wicklow coastline. 3. Kilcoole, south of the old railway station. 4. Broad Lough, north of Wicklow Town. 5. Wicklow Head, south of Wicklow Town. 6. Arklow Point. 7. Glen of the Downs and Devil's Glen, near Ashford. 8. Blessington Lake. 9. Derrybawn Wood and Glendalough National Park, near Laragh.

BIRDWATCHING BREAKS

Dublin/Wicklow

Summer

DAY ONE: A day trip to Ireland's Eye island is highly recommended. Licensed boats leave from Howth Harbour. There is a seabird colony with many species of birds including puffins and gannets. Coastal species will also be seen on the Island. Remember, sea-cliffs can be dangerous.

DAY TWO: Travel south to Wicklow. Go to Glendalough National Park, three kilometres west of the village of Laragh. An early start will allow you to practise bird-call identification. Good for warblers and some of our scarce-breeding song birds. If you are really dedicated, the dawn chorus in a woodland is an unforgettable experience. Then travel east to the beach at Kilcoole for seabirds, especially the rare little tern which usually breeds on the shingle beach. Do not disturb these birds. If time permits carry on to Wicklow Head where breeding seabirds, ravens and peregrines on the cliffs can be seen in safety.

Winter

DAY ONE: The Bull Island has enough ducks, geese and waders to keep any birdwatcher occupied for a full morning (or even a day). Try to arrange it for a day when the tide will be full at about midday. This will ensure very close views of most of the species to be seen. In the afternoon carry on to nearby Howth Head and explore the cliff walk and harbour for seagulls and other species.

DAY TWO: Travel south to Kilcoole for more winter visitors such as geese and waders. Broadlough and Blessington lake are also worth a visit to round off the weekend.

Wexford

Summer and Winter

A visit to the Wexford area at any time of the year is memorable and the beginner and expert alike will benefit from a trip to the Visitors' Centre on the OPW/IWC Wexford Wildfowl Reserve. It is open all year round. Opening times from 1 October to 15 April are from 10.00am to 5.00pm, and from 16 April to 30 September from 9.00am to 6.00pm. There are also weekend guides all year round and a phone call to the wardens at the reserve on 053-23129/Fax: 053-24785 will be a great help when planning your weekend trip to this top-class birdwatching county. Groups can be catered for.

Cork

Summer

One of the best spots for a summer break of a day, weekend or a month has to be Cape Clear. Check with the Cape Clear Co-op (Tel. 028-39119) for details of bed and breakfast and self-catering accommodation on the island. The Bird Observatory at the north harbour (where the ferry docks) provides self-catering accommodation. The warden is usually there from April to October. Book in advance, details from IWC. There is also a youth hostel. As well as many seabirds such as fulmar and gannet, coastal land birds such as peregrine and raven and migrants in spring and autumn, there is stunning scenery. Even on a day trip, check with the warden at the observatory about where to go and what to see. Ferries depart daily from Baltimore (Tel: 028-39159) and Schull.

Winter

Spend a weekend based in Cobh, twenty kilometres south-east of Cork. It is centrally located in Cork Harbour, internationally important for waterfowl. Accessible by train and car. For a walking weekend, Great Island on which Cobh is situated is ideal.

DAY ONE: Look for gulls and seabirds from the piers in the town, then go to IWC Cuskinny Marsh Nature Reserve, just two kilometres east, for good views of gulls, waterfowl and woodland birds all. Staying on the island, a visit to Belvelly and Rossleague, just four kilometres north of Cobh, at any time other than full tide will be rewarded by good views of waders and ducks. Over 100 species have been seen on Great Island in one day during January. Contact Cork tourist office for accommodation information.

DAY TWO: Travel to Rostellan lake and wood in the south-east corner of Cork Harbour, following the signposts to Midleton and then Whitegate. The lake on the right is reached after about nine kilometres. Check the lake for waterfowl and look out for kingfishers and also sparrowhawks in the wood. Then take the road back to Midleton and look for signposts on the left for Cloyne and then Ballycotton, about twenty kilometres east of Rostellan. Good for waterfowl and waders on the lake and beach to the east of the village. The pier in the village is a good place for gulls and other seabirds. Ballycotton is also one of the best places in Ireland for rare birds. It will keep you busy for a morning at least. Scenic village.

Note: The Lough in Cork City is excellent for close-up views of gulls and ducks. Beware, there are many feral and exotic bird species and a large flock of mute swans which are always looking for a piece of bread or a free meal.

Kerry

Summer

One of the most spectacular places to spend a day birdwatching in Ireland is the Skellig Islands. Get close views of a host of seabirds. Boat trips, which last the best part of a day, depart from Portmagee and Ballinskelligs. The best month for a visit is July (or June). Advanced booking of boat trips strongly recommended.

Winter

DAY ONE: Walk the footpath from Tralee to Blennerville along the River Lee estuary. Good views of common waders and gulls, rarer gulls also. At Blennerville Windmill scan the estuary for flocks of waders, including lapwings and golden plovers. Many of Kerry's rarer waders have been seen here.

DAY TWO: Killarney woodland walk. Start at Ross Castle, just outside Killarney town. Take the trail to the north of the castle. Many woodland species, including finches and wintering blackcaps and chiffchaffs. Ducks can be seen on the lake from the trail. This walk will keep the visitor busy for a morning.

Clare/Galway

Summer

A trip to Inishbofin in County Galway any time during the summer is both relaxing and enjoyable. Two of our rarest breeding birds, the corncrake and the corn bunting still breed there. Small numbers of seabirds and other coastal species in a beautiful setting. A ferry leaves from Cleggan near Clifden, west of Galway.

Winter

Galway Bay is both scenic and a very easy place from which to birdwatch. A weekend based in Galway City is highly recommended.

DAY ONE: Start at New Quay near Ballyvaughan, checking the bay for divers, grebes and diving ducks. Ask here or to the east at Kinvarra for directions to Aughinish causeway and check the bay slowly. Drive towards Galway City and stop for directions to Tawin Island. Again take your time, watching out for geese.

DAY TWO: Go to the Claddagh in Galway City and walk out to Nimmo's Pier, where the Corrib river flows into Galway Bay. Check the area for gulls and ducks. Don't be surprised if you meet other birdwatchers here. It is an excellent place to see scarce and rare gulls. Travel to Salthill and check the beach and rocky outcrops for waders. Travelling north to Lough Corrib on the Headford road, at the village of Ballindooly turn left and travel to the lake shore at Angliham marble quarries. Check the lake for ducks.

Donegal

Between March and October, Liz and Ralph Sheppard lead wildlife holidays in Dunfanaghy (074-36208). Full board includes packed lunch, and a minibus is provided. Birds include northern specialities such as long-tailed duck, all species of Irish geese, choughs, etc. in March or October. There are plenty of nesting seabirds, as well as corncrakes, ring ouzels, a wealth of wildflowers – all in stunning scenery.

The Sheppards also have at their own home two fully-equipped farm cottages for self-catering throughout the year. They are located at Carnowen, Raphoe (074-47129), and are central for many good wetlands in winter. The farm itself has a river with kingfishers and dippers and two recently-planted deciduous woods. Advice on where to go, guided outings and tuition on all branches of natural history are available.

Antrim

DAY ONE: Take a day trip in summer to the RSPB reserve on Rathlin Island, County Antrim, for spectacular views of sea and coastal birds, including puffins, peregrines, choughs and buzzards. June is the best month and booking with the RSPB warden is essential (Tel. 02657-63935). Boats leave from Ballycastle.

DAY TWO: Explore the Antrim Hills. Visit Craigy Wood, just west of Cushendun, about fifteen kilometres south-east of Ballycastle. It is a National Trust Reserve. Contact the National Trust at 0238-510721. Breen Oakwood, which is a National Nature Reserve, is also worth visiting. It is off the Armoy-Glenshesk-Ballycastle Road.

Down

Winter

Stay at Newtownards, County Down. Strangford Lough will provide more than enough birds to fill a weekend. The road on the eastern shore of the Lough, south to Portaferry, will give good views of the wildfowl and waders in places. Grey Abbey should not be missed. It is especially good for geese and ducks. A visit should also be made to the Wildfowl and Wetland Centre at Castle Espie (Tel. 0247-874146), not far from Newtownards and signposted from the A22 Comber to Killyleagh and Downpatrick road. Educational and visitor facilities. Good for geese, ducks and woodland birds.

Armagh

The Lough Neagh Discovery Centre is well worth visiting. It is located on the south-east corner of Lough Neagh, seven kilometres from Lurgan. For details contact the Discovery Centre at Craigavon (Tel. 0762-322205).

Important: Take plenty of time at each site on your trips. Many birds will be missed on brief visits.

GLOSSARY

BINS/BINOS/BINOCKS – birdwatchers' terms for binoculars.

BIRDER/BIRDING – birdwatcher/bird-watching.

BIRD OF PREY – a term used to describe any bird species that eats birds, mammals and other higher vertebrates. Usually includes the owls. See also 'raptor'.

BIRD RACE – usually a team event where each team tries to see or hear as many different species of bird as possible in a set period, usually twenty-four hours, and often within set boundaries. 'Birdwatch race' would be a more accurate title.

DIP – to dip in birdwatching is to miss seeing a new, rare or scarce species. You dipped or dipped out by not seeing the bird.

FALL – this is when a large number of migrant birds arrive at a location at the one time. For example at Cape Clear in autumn, hundreds of meadow pipits or goldcrests will arrive on the island overnight, in suitable weather conditions. This is referred to as a 'fall' of migrants.

FIRST-/SECOND-/THIRD-... WINTER or SUMMER – some species such as the gulls take two to four years to reach adult plumage. During this period they can be aged on their plumage appearance. Therefore a herring gull in its first winter after hatching can be specifically identified as a 'first winter herring gull'.

JIZZ – a combination of characteristics which identify a living bird, but which may not be distinguished individually.

ON PASSAGE – refers to a bird seen during migration. See also 'passage migrant'.

PASSAGE MIGRANT – a bird that is seen in Ireland while migrating from its winter to summer areas and vice versa.

PASSERINE – a bird belonging to the order of passeriformes or perching birds.

PELAGIC – usually means far from land on the open ocean. Birdwatchers will sometimes travel far out to sea on a boat to observe oceanic or pelagic seabirds that rarely come close enough to land to be seen. Often referred to as 'going on a pelagic'.

PHYLLOSC – a term used when a small warbler showing characteristics of the family phylloscopus is seen but cannot be specifically identified. Other warbler families which are often abbreviated include hippolais (hippo), and acrocephalus (acro).

RAPTOR – a term used to describe an unspecifically identified hawk, falcon, eagle or buzzard, but not usually owls.

RINGING – the act of placing a very light metal ring on a bird, by a highly trained and licensed bird ringer. The birds are usually caught in very fine nets called 'mist nets' which do not harm them.

SCOPE – telescope.

SEA WATCHING – observing seabird movements from headlands and offshore islands, often in wet and windy conditions.

SUMMER/WINTER – these terms do not always follow the dictionary definition. For example, winter often refers to the period from October to the end of March, especially when discussing 'winter visitors' such as ducks, geese and waders. Likewise, summer can refer to the period from late March to the end of August when discussing 'summer visitors' such as terns and swallows.

TICK – if you see a new species it is called a 'tick' because you tick it off on your checklist of birds.

TWITCHER – someone who is interested in rare or scarce birds, sometimes travelling long distances at short notice to try and see a species which they have never seen before and add it to their list.

VAGRANT – a bird species that is scarce or rare, usually blown off course on migration.

WADERS – a group of birds that inhabit the water's edge, often wading in water and feeding on worms and small animals that live in mud or sand.

WARBLERS – a group of small, plain-looking birds that are highly migratory and usually eat insects. Some species in the group are so similar in appearance that they can only be separated by close examination in the hand.

WESTERN PALEARCTIC – the geographical region in which the island of Ireland is situated. This region stretches from the Azores to the Ural mountains and from north Africa to the Arctic.

WRECK – Similar to a fall but involves seabirds, usually auks, which are blown inland after strong gales.

USEFUL ADDRESSES

Irish Wildbird Conservancy (IWC)
Ruttledge House,
8 Longford Place,
Monkstown, County Dublin.
Telephone: 01-2804322

Royal Society for the Protection of Birds
(RSPB Northern Ireland),
Belvoir Park Forest,
Belfast BT8 4QT.
Telephone: 0232-491547

The Environmental Information Service (ENFO),
17 St. Andrew's Street,
Dublin 2.
Telephone: 01-6793144

Irish Wildlife Federation,
132A East Wall Road, Dublin 3.
Telephone: 01-366821

Irish Peatland Conservation Council,
195 Pearse Street, Dublin 2.

National Trust for Northern Ireland,
Rowallane House, Saintfield,
Ballynahinch, Co. Down.
Telephone: 0238-510721

National Parks and Wildlife Service,
Office of Public Works,
51 St. Stephen's Green, Dublin 2.
Telephone: 01-6613111

Department of the Environment for Northern Ireland
(Countryside and Wildlife Branch),
Calvert House,
23 Castle Place,
Belfast BT1 1FY.
Telephone: 0232-230560

An Taisce,
Tailors' Hall,
Back Lane,
Dublin 8.
Telephone: 01-541786

RECOMMENDED BOOKS, TAPES, CDs AND VIDEOS

Children's books

Usborne Series

Well-produced series of books on all aspects of natural history, including birds. Economically priced.

Young Ornithologist's Guides
published by Hamlyn

A series of slim volumes covering various aspects of bird study.

Identification

Ireland

Pocket Guide to Birds
G. Darcy

Handy-sized identification guide illustrating birds in Ireland.

Complete Guide to Ireland's Birds
E. Dempsey & M. O'Clery

Reference guide for identifying Ireland's common and rare birds.

Europe

The Mitchell Beazley Birdwatcher's Pocket Guide
Peter Hayman

Pocket guide with numerous illustrations of each species.

A Field Guide to the Birds of Britain and Europe
Roger Peterson, Guy Mountfort and P.A.D. Hollom

A classic guide to Europe's birds. Not quite pocket-sized.

Birds of Europe with North Africa and the Middle East
Lars Jonsson.

A beautifully illustrated guide to the birds of Europe and beyond. Definitely not pocket-sized!

Photographic Guide to the Birds of Britain and Europe
Delin and Svensson.

Probably the best photographic guide available on European birds. An ideal companion volume for those guides listed above.

Bird Distribution

The Atlas of Wintering Birds of Britain and Ireland
Peter Lack

A large reference book with species accounts and showing distribution maps of all species wintering in Britain and Ireland between the winters of 1981/82 and 1983/84.

The New Atlas of Breeding Birds in Britain and Ireland: 1988-1991
D.W. Gibbons et al.

Essential sister companion to the last book. Brilliantly illustrated species accounts and detailed abundance and distribution maps of all the breeding birds in Britain and Ireland during 1988-1991.

Ireland's Wetland Wealth
Ralph Sheppard

Results of the Winter Wetlands Survey, surveying waterfowl during the three seasons 1984/85 to 1986/87.

Proof of the valuable contribution that amateurs can make to our understanding of birds.

Site Guides

Where to Watch birds in Ireland
Clive Hutchinson

Detailed maps and advice on the best birdwatching locations in Ireland.

Essential companion for planning a visit to any part of Ireland.

First Aid

St. Tiggywinkle's Wildcare Handbook
Les Stocker
A very comprehensive, practical reference book on the care of birds and other animals.

Bird Sounds

All the Bird Songs of Britain and Europe
J. Roche
A four-cassette/CD set of all the songs and calls of birds in Europe. Notes included and announcement of each species.

Our Favourite Garden Birds
Recording of garden birds. Includes species not found in Irish gardens.

Annual Bird Reports

Irish Birds
published by the IWC
Contains many papers on all aspects of Irish ornithology. Also includes an annual bird report listing rare and note-worthy observations of birds.

Northern Ireland Bird Report
Similar format to *Irish Birds*.

Regional and County Reports.

Cape Clear Bird Report, Cork Bird Report, Irish East Coast Bird Report, Wexford Bird Report
All are very valuable for detailed accounts of birds, at local and county level. Usually produced annually.

Videos

There are many videos on birds and birdwatching on the market which are suitable for home or school.

Paul Doherty's Video Guide to Gulls, Wildfowl and Waders
Narrated by Bill Oddie
An excellent reference for what can be a very confusing group of birds.

Gardening: Strictly for the Birds.
Shows how to make your garden a haven for birds.

BBC Guide to Garden Birds
Deals exclusively with birds to be seen in the garden or near the home. Includes some species not found in Ireland.

RSPB Educational Videos
Covers various topics such as migration, flight, nests, etc. Designed for the classroom.

These titles and more are available through the IWC 'Wings' Gift Shop at 8 Longford Place, Monkstown, Co. Dublin. Tel. 01-280 4322.

BIBLIOGRAPHY

Armstrong E.A., *The Folklore of Birds* (London, 1958)

Campbell B. & Lack E., *A Dictionary of Birds* (Calton, 1985)

Cooper Foster J., *Ulster Folklore* (Belfast, 951)

Gibbons et al., *The New Atlas of Breeding Birds in Britain and Ireland 1988-1991* (Calton, 1993)

Ginn H.B. & Melville D.S., *Moult in Birds* (Tring, 1983)

Harrison C., *A Field Guide to the Nests, Eggs and Nestlings of British and European Birds* (London, 1975)

Hutchinson C.D., *Watching Birds in Ireland* (Dublin, 1986)

Hutchinson C.D., *Birds in Ireland* (Calton, 1989)

Hutchinson C.D., *Where to Watch Birds in Ireland* (Dublin, 1994)

Jonsson L., *Birds of Europe with North Africa and the Middle East* (London, 1992)

Joyce P.W., *Irish Names of Places, Vol. I* (London, *circa* 1890)

Lack P., *The Atlas of Wintering Birds in Britain and Ireland* (Calton, 1986)

Moriarty C., *A Guide to Irish Birds* (Cork, 1967)

Prater et al., *Guide to the Identification and Ageing of Holarctic Waders* (Tring, 1977)

Pemberton J., *The Birdwatcher's Yearbook and Diary 1993* (Buckingham, 1992)

An Rionn Oideachais, *Ainmeacha Plandaí agus Ainmhithe* (Dublin, 1978)

Ruttledge R.F., *A List of the Birds of Ireland* (Dublin, 1975)

Soper T., *The Bird Table Book* (London, 1986, 5th Ed.)

Stocker L., *St. Tiggywinkle's Wildcare Handbook* (London, 1992)

Various Editors, *Irish Birds 1977-1993* (Dublin).

Irish Wildbird Conservancy

– Working for Ireland's Birds –

IWC IS THE LARGEST INDEPENDENT voluntary conservation organisation in Ireland, with over 4,000 members and 23 branches nationwide.

IWC'S PRIMARY OBJECTIVE is the conservation of wild birds and the protection of Ireland's natural habitats. Through Birdlife International, we represent Irish birdwatchers' interests worldwide.

As a member of the Irish Wildbird Conservancy you would be assisting in this vital work – helping wild birds to thrive, free in their natural environment.

IWC MEMBERSHIP GIVES YOU:

- A *free* new membership pack

- Entry to IWC lectures and outings all around the country

- Our quarterly magazine – IWC NEWS – packed with fascinating articles and photographs of birds.

In fact, a year's IWC membership makes a great gift too!

**Irish Wildbird Conservancy,
8 Longford Place,
Monkstown, Co. Dublin
Phone (01) 280 4322 Fax (01) 284 4407**

JOIN THE IWC – TODAY!